Cavalry in the Franco-Prussian War

Cavalry in the Franco-Prussian War

Actions of French Cavalry 1870
by Jean Jacques Théophile Bonie

Cavalry at Vionville & Mars-la-Tour
by Otto August Johannes Kaehler

LEONAUR

Cavalry in the Franco-Prussian War
Actions of French Cavalry 1870 by Jean Jacques Théophile Bonie
Cavalry at Vionville & Mars-la-Tour by Otto August Johannes Kaehler

First published under the title
Cavalry Studies from Two Great Wars

Leonaur is an imprint of Oakpast Ltd

Copyright in this form © 2010 Oakpast Ltd

ISBN: 978-0-85706-379-3 (hardcover)
ISBN: 978-0-85706-380-9 (softcover)

http://www.leonaur.com

Publisher's Notes

Contents

Original Editor's Preface

The work of Colonel (now General) Bonie appeared very soon after the close of the Franco-German War, having been written, as it were, in the smoke of battle. In this respect it differs materially from the book of Major Kaehler, which is a recent production, and now makes its appearance in English for the first time. While Kaehler, unlike Bonie, does not write as an eye-witness and with the experience of an actual participator in the events described, he has had the advantage of historical researches which were not available to the French author, and though his book is naturally a less vivid picture, it can doubtless lay claim to greater historical accuracy than that of its companion.

U. S. Infantry and Cavalry School,
Fort Leavenworth, Kansas.
February 17, 1896.

Actions of French Cavalry 1870

Jean Jacques Théophile Bonie

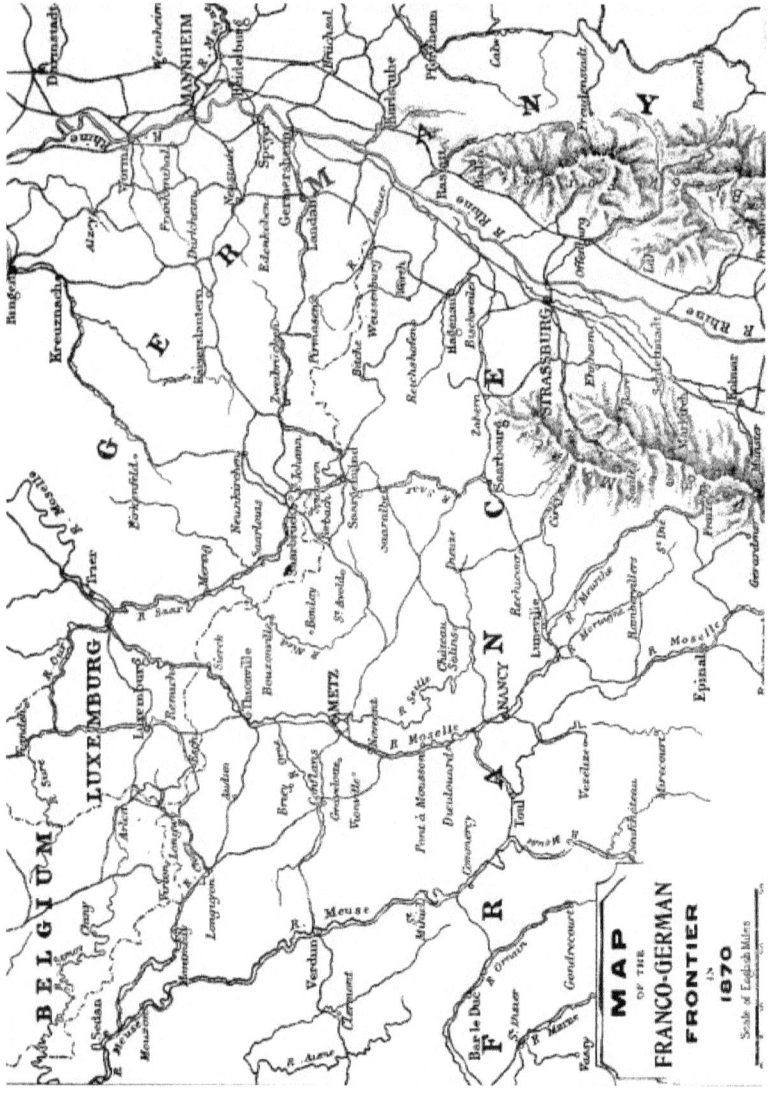

FRANCO-GER-
MAN FRONTIER
1870

Preface

For some years past public opinion has been a good deal occupied with the influence that would be exercised on cavalry by the greatly increased importance of infantry and artillery. Discussions on this subject, at first very unfavourable to cavalry, greatly diminished the prestige of that arm; soon afterwards a sort of reaction set in, and it was allowed that, as formerly, it was an indispensable portion of an army, only, however, on the condition that it should understand how to accommodate itself to *modern* changes. The necessity for a change was of the greatest importance, considering the complete revolution that was taking place in all European armies, in everything that related to warfare.

Unfortunately, the committee appointed to consider the necessary changes, instead of setting to work vigorously, was more inclined to let things remain in *statu quo*, and came to the conclusion that both the regulations and system of tactics approved of in 1829 were perfect for 1869.

In the midst of this indifference war suddenly broke out, and we were obliged to appear on the field of battle with our old ideas and our old mistakes. In the course of this work we shall find the cavalry, as formerly in its best days, full of chivalrous devotion, having learnt nothing, it is true, but at the same time not forgetful of its past bravery and patriotism.

Generally injudiciously employed in this last war, our cavalry has nevertheless, in spite of the conviction that they were riding to a certain and useless death, always charged with valour and determination. Unhappily, the blood that has been so generously poured out has served merely to save the honour of our arms, without always reaping the reward of victory.

Our sworn enemy, if less brilliant in this respect, has at any rate shown himself more practical. Carrying on his preparations with secrecy, he burst upon us with all the greater force and overwhelmed us. Whilst we were occupied in disputing as to the utility of cavalry, he, on the other hand, casting aside prejudice, busied himself in perfecting that branch of the service; in this manner the weight of cavalry in this campaign has been such that to it Prussia owes, for the most part, her unparalleled successes, and to prove this we will let facts speak for themselves.

All will acknowledge that the French cavalry did all that courage could do, but in other and more important points it was found wanting. From this it seems certain that the instruction imparted to the cavalry should undergo important modifications. We shall endeavour to show what these modifications should be, taking into consideration the experience gained by the events of the late war. A diligent study of the part played by the enemy's cavalry and our own, more surely than any theory, will point out to us the course to pursue. Such is the object of this volume. It is the faithful story of what befell the cavalry in the War of 1870.

Note. In the following translation *peloton* has been rendered troop, and the distances given in the original in metres have been expressed approximately in yards.

PART 1

CHAPTER 1

Mobilization of the Cavalry

As soon as war had been formally declared against Prussia, the various cavalry regiments received the order to mobilize. Immediately the vices of our organization were brought to light, and, in spite of all efforts, our zeal failed to contend successfully against impossibilities. It is evident that during peace regiments cannot be kept up to a war footing; such a system would be ruinous. But, since this is the case, there is all the more reason that a system should be adopted which should enable the cavalry to receive, on the shortest notice, supplies of men and horses sufficient to carry the total to a war strength; otherwise the cavalry, which ought to precede the army in order to obtain intelligence, will, on the contrary, be the last ready, and, instead of being the vanguard, will be the rearguard.

At the commencement of this war we not only had no reserves of horses, but a portion of our effective strength was composed of four-year-old remounts. Thus it was that with the greatest difficulty we only succeeded in getting together four squadrons per regiment, of one hundred and two horses each, which strength, the smallest with which one can take the field, was soon lessened by a few days of hard work.

As the commissariat stores were empty, we were deficient in mess tins, cans, kettles, and other necessaries for camp life. On fresh arrivals indenting for what was requisite, they were informed that their predecessors had taken everything, that application had been made to Paris, and that they must wait for fresh supplies. Time passed, nothing arrived, and officers, as well as men, were obliged to march without the most necessary articles. The same want of preparation was the case in the medical department; they were only just beginning to get the ambulance into working order. Finally, as the generals had to get the scattered regiments they were to command together from all sorts of places, the marches and counter-marches were interminable; all this time the enemy boldly advanced. Everybody kept repeating that we had two days' start of the enemy; only, as the latter was already on our frontier, the facts contradicted the report, and a vague idea got abroad that our information was not of the best, and that we were but badly prepared for a gigantic struggle, and that already we had begun in a feeble manner.

It was now, however, too late to talk; war was declared, and, ready or not, we had only one thing to do *viz.*, to do our duty to the best of our ability; so, as is usual in such cases, one hoped for the best, and, full of confidence, we advanced to meet the enemy.

CHAPTER 2

Positions of the Armies

At the commencement of hostilities, the French Army was *echeloned* along the frontier, with a front of about one hundred miles; the whole forming an angle of which Wissembourg formed the apex, and Strasbourg and Thionville two points at the base. The Germans advanced against us in three bodies; the first, commanded by Steinmetz, held a position behind the Sarre; the second, under the command of Prince Frederick Charles, was in the valley of the Moselle; and the third, which had for its chief the Crown Prince of Prussia, rested on Rastadt. These three armies, more concentrated than ours, could naturally assume the offensive as soon as they had pierced our thin line.

It was necessary for them, in order to do this with safety, to push their patrols and scouts well ahead, and get the best information possible. For some years Prussia had been teaching her cavalry to perform this delicate portion of their duties with intelligence. In 1866 the cavalry did but little; but, learning from the experience gained in that war how important a mission it had to fill for the future, and how greatly its sphere of action had been enlarged by the new system of artillery tactics, it set itself to learn how to act from long distances, to watch us with unceasing vigilance, and to serve as a curtain to the rest of the army; in short, to practice how to mask one's own movements whilst finding out everything concerning the enemy.

In order to obtain the above results, the first thing necessary is to be perfectly acquainted with the country one is going to work over. How, it may be asked, is one to pass rapidly along the roads with a chance of doing so successfully, if one is obliged to waste one's time in trying different ways, and constantly changing the direction of the march? This art the enemy has brought to perfection. It is as easy for them to read a map as an open book; with us, on the other hand, it is

15

like wandering in a fog. At the last moment an outline map of Germany had been served out to a few officers; as for a map of our own country, nobody thought of it.

Everybody was supposed to be perfectly acquainted with his own country; and, as it is impossible to remember all the roads in France, our cavalry was obliged to trust to chance, whilst the enemy's pushed on without hesitation. Thus we began the war by discovering one of the mistakes in the practical teaching imparted to us, and the result was a disadvantage that the most brilliant courage was unable to counterbalance.

Chapter 3

Preliminary Operations

From the very commencement the German cavalry, by its daring preliminary operations on our eastern frontiers, gave us proofs of its intelligence and skill. With unparalleled audacity, it pushed across the boundary. Choosing a few men, to the number of five or six together, they pushed them forward to gain intelligence, cut telegraph wires, etc., and, by their sudden appearances, strike terror into the inhabitants.

Towards the end of July the first cavalry skirmishes took place. On the 28th there was an affair to the northeast of Sarreguemines, close to the bridge over the Blies. The same night some Bavarian *chasseurs* pushed forward in order to break up the line of railway from Sarreguemines to Haguenau. Every day the same thing—like an irritating fly, that is driven away only to return the next moment—the enemy's cavalry could not be laid hold of. They even pushed their audacity so far as to dismount and enter the inns. It was in this way that a reconnaissance made, close to Niederbronn, by some of the Baden cavalry, was surprised and attacked by our men. Three officers of the Baden dragoons, one of them an Englishman, were killed.

But what did this signify, provided one of the party escaped to tell the tale of what he had seen? The object for which the operation had been undertaken was accomplished. It is thus that the German cavalry made their *début* in this war; *viz.*, in showing, from the first, an unlimited confidence in the dash of their men, and in the staying powers of their horses.

Astonished by these manoeuvres, our cavalry endeavoured to do likewise, but failed, owing to their imperfect knowledge of the country, and were obliged to confine themselves to merely posting *vedettes* along the frontier. A few scouts sent ahead at the right moment would have sufficed to end this continued annoyance. Instead, however, we thought fit to employ troops, squadrons, and even regiments, to watch the country. Thus we exemplified the old proverb of the lion and the gnat, and opposed stratagem with force, and in so doing we used up the cavalry told off for this duty to no purpose, ere a battle had taken place.

At the end of July the infantry divisions placed under the orders of Marshal MacMahon left Strasbourg in order to occupy their destined positions, and found, on arrival, their divisional cavalry waiting for them. The cavalry was formed in two divisions the first, under the command of General Duhesme, consisted of the Brigades Septeuil (3rd Hussars, 11th Chasseurs), Nansouty (10th Dragoons, 2nd and 6th Lancers), and Michel (8th and 9th Cuirassiers); the second division was commanded by General de Bonnemain, and consisted of the Brigades Girard (1st and 4th Cuirassiers) and Brauer (2nd and 3rd Cuirassiers). Of these eleven regiments, six formed the reserve, the seventh was wanting and did not arrive, whilst the four others were detached to do duty with infantry, and were the divisional cavalry.

CHAPTER 4

Divisional Cavalry

It is now necessary to discuss the *rôle* of this cavalry, for it was an experiment, and one on which the greatest expectation of happy results was founded. As a matter of theory, the plan seemed seductive and excellent. The cavalry, sheltered at the commencement of an action behind inequalities of ground, were, it was said, to watch their opportunity, and throw themselves upon the enemy already shaken by the infantry; then, should this prove successful, to pursue, or, if they experienced a check, to retire quickly to the place from whence they came.

So much for theory. Practice has not justified this manner of employing us; shells search every nook and corner, and the shelter afforded by the inequalities of ground was almost imaginary. As for throwing oneself upon the enemy seeing that their artillery, placed in positions inaccessible to cavalry, commenced to play upon us from a distance of from three to four thousand yards it was useless to think of it.

Having been personally attached to an infantry division, I studied, with interest, how this system worked, and found that, with the exception of a little scouting, there was literally nothing for the remainder of the regiment to do, and we were generally in the way.

The moment the cavalry approached the general, the enemy, invariably on the *qui vive*, sent such a shower of bullets that the escort had to be much decreased in order to avoid turning the general into a living target.

In addition to all this, let us add that first the infantry general gave us an order, then the cavalry general, who did not like being set aside, gave another, and these continual changes of orders brought about a state of incertitude extremely prejudicial to carrying out an order properly.

In short, supposing you have a cavalry like ours, inferior in number to the enemy's, a regiment for a division of infantry is too large a proportion. One or two squadrons would be ample, as their real business is to keep in constant communication the various links of the military chain which constitutes the line of battle.

As for divisional cavalry scouting, it can only do so in a very partial and local manner. We acted according to our theory in this war, and we have no reason to congratulate ourselves on the way it worked in practice.

Instead of employing a portion of the cavalry specially to gain intelligence, we thought it better to let each infantry division have its own cavalry, and these acting each in its own way, the whole front would be covered by the reunion of the scattered portions. But this isolated way of arranging matters does not answer, for if one portion is found wanting, the rest of the line is not aware of it, and the whole is compromised. We shall see how this was the case on the 4th August. The divisions were separated and the most distant was annihilated without any aid having been afforded to it.

The Prussians do not act in this manner. From the right to the left every portion is in communication, so that if anything happens, it is known all along the front; as soon as contact with the enemy is established, it is never again lost; thus the smallest movements are known, and immediately the weak spot is discovered it is attacked. It was thus that, certain of what they were attempting, they surprised us at Wissembourg.[1]

---

1. As this work is intended for cavalry, only sufficient will be said of the other two arms to show how the cavalry came on the scene.

CHAPTER 5

Battle of Wissembourg

On the 4th August our troops were encamped as follows: The 2nd division (Gen. Douai), in front, was at Wissembourg; the 1st division (Gen. Ducrot) at Woerth; the 3rd (Gen. Raoult) was in rear of it; and the 4th (Gen. de Lartigues) had only marched from Strasbourg at four o'clock that morning *en route* for Haguenau. The cavalry occupied Soultz, Seltz, Haguenau, and Brumath. Taking into consideration these positions, which had the disadvantage of being a good deal separated, the part that should have been played by an active and intelligently instructed force of cavalry is easy to trace; first to scout and cover the leading division in such a manner as to render a surprise impossible, for otherwise its isolation rendered a disaster extremely probable; next, to establish a chain of communication between the other divisions, so as to enable them to get timely notice to march to the help of the one attacked.

From theory let us turn to fact.

The second division, not warned of coming danger, was surprised and overwhelmed by the enemy, who appeared with much larger forces, and crushed our unfortunate soldiers with their superior artillery; seven thousand men were pitted against thirty-five thousand; General Douai came up in haste, and had only time to call to his escort as he passed in front of the cavalry at a gallop; a few minutes later he was killed in endeavouring to encourage his men already decimated, thus preferring a soldier's death on the field of battle to retreat.

The other divisions, ignorant of what was going on, were unable to come to the rescue of this fraction of our army which was fighting with such desperation. This handful of men was opposed to a whole *corps d'armee*, and was finally annihilated. The 50th and 74th regiments almost ceased to exist. The Brigade Septeuil, though eagerly waiting, failed to find an opportunity of charging, owing to the bad ground, and our camp was seized upon by the enemy's cavalry, who took possession of the baggage.

Towards two o'clock fighting ceased, and the remains of the 2nd division retired on Lembach.

This recital renders useless all comment on our manner of employing divisional cavalry. Its negative role only stands out too prominently, and it would be painful to dwell further on this subject.

After this action the Prussians pushed forward, following close on our retreating troops, without, however, attacking them, owing to the difficulties in the ground, and so, during the night of the 5th 6th, the 1st *corps d'armee* found itself concentrated on the heights close to Reichshoffen and Froeschwiller. The weather was dreadful; a storm burst, and the rain fell in torrents, converting the plains on which were encamped into marshes; in spite of the weather, the enemy's *vedettes* never lost sight of us; with ceaseless vigilance they studied our position, and ascertained our weakness in point of numbers, and thus enabled their own side to make all necessary arrangements for the morrow's engagement.

CHAPTER 6

Battle of Woerth

On the 6th August the *corps d'armee* of Marshal MacMahon was posted on the eastern slope of the Vosges; it occupied the heights that lie between Froeschwiller and Woerth, Elsashausen and Gunstett. The left extended as far as the valley of Jaegerthal, and the 4th division formed a disconnected line with the 3rd on the right. This was the weak point, as it could be turned. For this reason the Brigade Michel (8th and 9th Cuirassiers) was placed as a support behind this flank. The cavalry division (General de Bonnemain, 1st, 2nd, 3rd, 4th Cuirassiers) was placed in reserve, behind the 2nd infantry division, as also was the Brigade Septeuil (3rd Hussars and 11th Chasseurs).

The army of the Crown Prince was so disposed as to attack simultaneously at three points. The position it took up was exceedingly strong, and admirably defended by artillery posted on ridges commanding our lines; the form of the enemy's line was convex, with the Bavarians on the right, the Würtembergers on the left, and the Prussians in the centre. The cavalry was at Soultz.

At daybreak the enemy's outposts opened fire. The French cavalry not having obtained any information, Marshal MacMahon was left in ignorance of the fact that during the night the enemy's forces had been tripled, and believing it a simple reconnaissance, he accepted the battle.

Our left flank was attacked by the Bavarians, who held the wood on the right of Neerwiller. In the centre and right the Germans opened a formidable artillery fire. Towards eleven o'clock, fourteen batteries were firing into Woerth, and the enemy's infantry began to advance in order to seize upon it.

Women and children, frightened out of their senses, came asking for succour, and saying that the enemy had already penetrated into the streets; the *zouaves* and *turcos* now appeared on the scene. We could see them descend the incline, and cross the fields with as much order and regularity as on parade. A shower of bullets was poured on them, and though men fell on all sides, the intervals were closed and they still continued their onward course. On arriving at the village, the *turcos* entered the streets with a yell. A desperate hand-to-hand struggle took place here; the front ranks were mowed down by the musketry, dead bodies were heaped one on another, still every foot of ground was disputed, and our men died rather than yield; eventually, however, overcome by superior numbers, they were forced to give way.

About the same time Gunstett was taken. The Baden division now began to advance, and the Würtembergers moved up in support; the enemy were moving on Froeschwiller, and their whole army commenced an onward movement; Marshal MacMahon, in person, directed our columns to advance into the thickest of the danger, but the loss was too great, and they were unable to persevere. It now became necessary to call all our forces to our aid; accordingly General de Bonnemain received the order to bring up his cavalry.

The same morning, on arriving on the *plateau* of Froeschwiller, this division had been drawn up in four lines, at half distance. As it was not intended to employ this division at the commencement of the action, they were placed under the shelter of a hollow in the ground (the same in which is the source of the Eberbach) and at first were protected from the enemy's fire. About 11 o'clock the shells began to fall in great numbers, killing men and horses, right and left. The division now took ground to its right and rested on a wood. In front the ground was broken and full of ravines.

On the left there was sufficient space to form up in two lines. About 1:30 the Marshal sent for a brigade, and the 1st brigade received the order to advance, which they accordingly did, along a hollow to the right front. The 2nd brigade also inclined to its right; both brigades were in close column. The 1st brigade (1st and 4th Cuirassiers) was right in front, and leading towards the village of Sparsbach.

In front of the cavalry, and rather on their left, the infantry were endeavouring to hold their ground. As soon as the position became untenable, the cavalry attacked. Unfortunately, the ground was unfavourable, and, in addition to this, it was impossible to get at the enemy, as they were posted in hop-fields and vineyards, surrounded with palisades; for these reasons the charge was absurd, as nothing could be gained and none of the enemy reached. In spite of all this, their courage rose equal to the danger, and without the least hesitation the 1st Cuirassiers twice charged by squadrons in succession. As soon as they arrived at the top of the ridge they received the enemy's fire, and were forced to retire, with the loss of a large number of men and horses, and without having effected anything.

The 4th Cuirassiers were in support of this movement. In hopes of finding more favourable ground, they moved some 200 yards to their left, and, like their predecessors, charged by squadrons in succession. They advanced under fire about two-thirds of a mile through the hop-fields without seeing the enemy, and then received a heavy fire from a belt of wood. This regiment now returned, leaving the colonel on the field, and more cut up than the 1st.

The 2nd brigade now advanced and took the place of the 1st, and attacked to its front, over worse ground than the latter had done. In addition to the hop-fields, they had in front of them a ditch, lined with *chevaux de frise*, and forming an obstacle absolutely insurmountable. This charge was, therefore, bound to fail from the first.

The 2nd Cuirassiers charged by wings. They lost their colonel; 5 officers were killed, several wounded, and 129 men and 170 horses remained on the ground. In addition, 80 horses returned so badly wounded that they died in the next few days.

Lastly, the 3rd Cuirassiers were brought into action, and one wing charged. Their loss was equally severe. The colonel (De Lacarre) had his head carried away by a shot, and 7 officers and 70 men and horses were killed and wounded; in addition, several officers had their horses killed; one, a lieutenant, lost three. Thus terminated the first attempt to employ our cavalry on this campaign. The result of these charges, undertaken without proper forethought, was bloody and useless, as we were thrust forward into the open against an enemy always out of reach and often out of sight.

At the termination of these unsuccessful charges, the whole Prussian Army advanced. The villages of Froeschwiller and Woerth were on fire. Elsashausen was taken. At two o'clock we found ourselves opposed to such overwhelming numbers that it was impossible to maintain our ground. At this moment the enemy brought up fresh troops, and made a grand effort to secure success. Our right wing, not being secured, as has been already observed, could be turned. Already in the distance one could see the heads of the approaching columns. They wound over the hills and came on through the woods, nearer and nearer.

Regiment followed regiment, and finally they reached the lines they wished to reinforce. We were now taken both in front and flank; and our infantry, shaken by the fire, commenced to waver. A few stragglers caused some irregularity amongst those who still stood their ground, and confusion began to show itself.

There was now only one hope of saving these brave troops. The cavalry that had been posted in rear of the right was still fresh, and it was determined to employ them. We have already seen how one portion of this arm had behaved at the other end of the line; we shall now see the same bravery and devotion, only the result will be more disastrous. The ground was as follows: a small but steep hill in front; at its foot the cavalry awaited, under cover, the moment of action. The far side of the hill, equally steep, terminated in a plain, over which were scattered woods and hop-gardens. Further still lay the village of Morsbronn through which ran a narrow street leading into the fields, and having a sharp turn at the far end. Thus we have, as it were, an encircling frame, consisting of woods, houses swarming with infantry, and hop-gardens dotted with long poles, the whole affording the best of cover from which to shoot with ease and safety.

To charge, under these circumstances, is to rush to certain death, without a chance of success; each man is aware of this, but where duty and honour show the way they are willing to follow.

Up to the moment of charging, the 8th and 9th Cuirassiers were drawn up in two lines, perpendicular to the ravine. On their right rear was a small party of the 6th Lancers. This party did not belong to Michel's brigade; it was under the orders of the infantry general (De Lartigues), and was not intended to charge; it only did so by mistake.

The order to attack was given; how and by whom we will discuss further on. The regiments now changed front, and advanced parallel to the ravine. The 8th was formed in column of squadrons; the 9th was forced to diminish their front by having to pass between two clumps of trees; they then formed line to the front, with the exception of the 3rd squadron, and the party of the 6th, who were unable to change their formation.

As soon as General Michel was warned, he placed himself at the head of his brigade. The squadrons broke into a gallop, and the earth resounded to the tread of the horses, who kept quickening their pace. Unfortunately, the ground had not been reconnoitred, and it was supposed that it was necessary to charge over the open. The woods and hop-fields being impracticable, they rode through the intervals. The

8th led the way. The enemy waited immovable, took steady aim, and, as soon as the *cuirassed* line appeared at the proper distance, fired two volleys by word of command, followed by independent fire. The effect was murderous—two-thirds of the horses were hit, and staggered to the ground with their riders, thus forming a line of corpses. The remains of the regiment, passing through Morsbronn, gained the open.

The 9th Cuirassiers and 6th Lancers followed in support; but their advance was delayed by obstacles; the fire of the enemy was on this account more effective, and the whole mass was transformed into a confused mob of men and horses pressing one against another. They now got to the village, and were obliged to diminish their front to effect an entrance. A terrible and crushing fire was poured on them from the houses as they passed. They now found it was impossible to get through, as the end of the street was blocked, so they endeavoured to retreat; this attempt was unsuccessful, and, with the exception of a small number, all who were not killed were taken prisoners.

Such was the result of the second attempt with our cavalry on this day. It was even more disastrous than the first. On both occasions the bravery displayed was extreme; the results—*nil*. They started without knowing the object of the charge, and advanced without reconnoitring the ground in front of them, and, after losing heavily, fell back without having an opportunity of using their arms. The ground was covered with dead horses, and many a man owed his life to his *cuirass*. One could hear the bullets rattle like hail on the *cuirasses*, but none were pierced, and many dismounted men sought refuge in the woods.

The above is important, as it demonstrates the utility of the *cuirass*, and proves that it is not a thing of the past, as many assert; on the contrary, *cuirassiers* will always enter into the composition of cavalry for the future.[1]

After this futile disaster, nobody was willing to accept the responsibility of having ordered it. Some laid the responsibility on the cavalry commander, others on the infantry. As I was close to the latter during the last portion of this unfortunate day, I am in a position to state that I heard him ask several times, "What is the object of advancing three regiments? I only want one, to turn the enemy, and not to attack him

---

1. This was written some years ago, when the infantry rifle had by no means reached its present power. The *cuirass* is no longer retained in any army as a part of the field equipment, though it is still worn at ceremonies by some cavalry organizations.—A. L. W.

in front."

This false interpretation of an order or suggestion has happened at Mouzon, at Rézonville, and also at other places, and it is impossible to insist too strongly on the unfortunate consequences that have followed. When an *aide-de-camp* conveys the order to charge to a cavalry officer, he must not seem in too great a hurry, for the instinctive idea of the officer is to obey at once, without, as it were, taking time to reflect, as before all he is afraid of being accused of slowness or cowardice. All this is extremely natural, and if one is not careful to ascertain exactly the object to be gained and also to reconnoitre the ground, you entail the destruction of the troops engaged.

The charge at Woerth is an example. One regiment alone was wanted; three were pushed forward by mistake, and completely annihilated. We may as well now call attention to the 2nd Lancers as a regiment which suffered considerably. This regiment was left by the general, exposed to fire all day, without apparently an attempt to get them under cover. They lost their commanding officer (Col. Poissonnier) and eleven other officers without having charged.

One sees on all sides the same dash and the same want of skill in employing us. Efforts will, no doubt, be made to justify this series of errors, by asserting that the object for which the charges were undertaken was more or less obtained. It is necessary all this should be known, for otherwise how shall we profit by the rough lessons we have received? It is necessary that the history of this campaign should be truthfully and dispassionately written, and it is for this reason that we repeat "That the bravery of the cavalry was all that could be desired, but that their charges were futile." And of this, here is the proof: the object of these charges was to save the infantry, and give it time to recover itself and retreat.

A small portion of one regiment was indeed saved; but in order to effect this, we lost three times as many men and horses as, we saved foot soldiers. Where then was the advantage? As for saying we enabled the infantry to retreat, that is easily answered by the fact that there was no retreat, but a rout. One seems still to hear General de Lartigues calling to the *zouaves*, as he placed himself at their head, to follow him and die where they stood, and receiving the answer, "How are we to go on fighting? we have no more cartridges, and you can see how we are outnumbered."

There was neither terror nor despair, but everyone saw further resistance was hopeless. For eight hours we had fought like lions, and had afforded the spectacle of 35,000 standing up against 140,000, and for a long time keeping the day undecided. But there is a limit to all things, and the battle was decided before the cavalry charged; this sacrifice was therefore useless. Thus it will be seen that we saved nothing during the battle, nor did we protect the retreat, as the whole *corps d'armee* fled pell-mell. This is the truth about how we were employed in this battle.

After the final and useless effort of the cavalry, the enemy, finding that resistance ceased, attacked us on all sides. The fire caused such loss that the officers were unable any longer to maintain order, and the rout was complete; a storm of bullets followed on the track of our unfortunate soldiers, and swept away several at each discharge. We fell back in the direction of Reichshoffen, and as everyone wished to escape the carnage that was going on, the roads got blocked. At Niederbronn we were told to make for Saverne as a rallying-point, and, after crossing the railway, we mounted the low hills that surround that town, and commenced a long night march; officers and soldiers, generals, cannons and wagons, all in one disorderly mob, pushed along the road. In addition to the fatigue caused by the day's hard work, we now had to undergo the weariness brought on by continual stoppages.

The road was narrow, and anyone can picture to himself the confusion that would have reigned had the enemy, by continuing his fire, forced long lanes of carnage through the defenceless crowd. Night now came on and hid us from sight. How long the hours seemed, and what unpleasant reflections occurred to one, during this retreat, in which you could see before you but a few paces, and in which the silence was only broken by an occasional shot from a rifle discharged by accident, and which caused confusion by leading one to suppose that we were again attacked! Worn out by their exertions, many men now fell out and lay down in the fields and ditches by the roadside. Others, unwilling to be left behind, still struggled on, but, overcome with sleep, they staggered and leaned one against the other.

In this manner we marched some twelve leagues, an enormous distance for tired and hungry men who had fought all day. Between midnight and 1 a. m., some of the cavalry reached Saverne, and by degrees the remains of the *corps d'armee* reached this place. Happily, we were unmolested on this march, for, as we were without either front or rear guard or flankers, had the enemy pursued us vigorously, they must have completed our ruin. But the Prussians committed the terrible mistake of not employing properly their numerous and excellent cavalry, and this want of activity after the battle of Woerth, which arose perhaps from being unaware how great a victory they had obtained, allowed Marshal MacMahon to save the remnants of his disorganized force, and retreat across the Vosges in something like order.

After having committed the error of not exterminating us on the spot, the Prussians sent scouts to follow us up. These, as soon as they reached Niederbronn, captured our treasure, and from that moment displayed the greatest persistence and intelligence in the pursuit. The Prussian cavalry has a system of scouting very far superior on service to our own. They pushed ahead long distances with the greatest rapidity and daring, and the glory of ensuring the general success of their operations is entirely due to them. They search the villages, woods, by-paths—in short, the whole country, in such a complete and efficient manner that the troops in rear are enabled to make every arrangement and act without hesitation.

This manner of operating was unknown to us, and during peace we entered into mimic warfare with indifference and want of interest in the work. For this reason we were always surprised, and to it may be attributed many of our disasters. This fact will appear clearly in the record of our retreat, and by the contrast thus established between our cavalry and the Prussian, one will be able to judge which army has the best method of imparting drill and instruction.

During the whole of the night between the 6th and 7th August, the cavalry of the 1st *corps d'armee* kept arriving at Saverne, and by 8 a. m. nearly the whole had come up. We now set to work to restore order, when suddenly the parade call sounded; without being able to rest ourselves after the previous day's fatigues, we had to mount and proceed along the road which leads from Saverne across the Vosges.

The line of retreat we were ordered to follow was to proceed by Phalsbourg to Sarrebourg; and as we marched, our thoughts were occupied in considering how we were to live, as the enemy's cavalry had captured everything at the Battles of Wissembourg and Froeschwiller; they had even obtained possession of our carriages and led horses. As nothing was issued, and as we had neither clothes, tents, nor cooking-utensils, it was a difficult problem how we were to get on. Fortunately, the peasantry along the road gave us bread and wine; we excited their sympathy, as they were aware that we had fought with courage.

As soon as we got to Sarrebourg, the regiments were re-formed, and we sent in the returns of killed and wounded; according to these, the loss was exceptionally heavy. The generals now resumed command of their divisions and brigades, and as no one imagined we should abandon Alsace without an effort, we held ourselves in readiness for an offensive movement, when, about midday on the 8th, we received the order to saddle and bridle. We were now given to understand that the enemy's cavalry was in sight.

The fact was the enemy's advanced scouts were taken for the heads of strong columns, and immediately we again retreated. From this time until we reached Lunéville, their advanced parties watched us ceaselessly. By their system of having a continuous line of communication kept up by their cavalry, their main body always received the best information regarding our positions—when we marched and where we halted—and as they carried on their observations from some distance, and kept continually appearing and then disappearing, only to return, they kept us in a state of constant anxiety. Instead of acting in a similar manner, our cavalry was left in unwieldy masses, which rendered no service, either by protecting our own army or in any other way.

On the 10th we got to Lunéville, where we hoped to obtain the camp equipment we stood in need of. In fact, we were informed that now there would be regular issues of hay and corn for our horses, and (luxuries that we had almost forgotten) of meat, sugar, and coffee for ourselves. The men, on this, recovered their spirits, lit fires, set to work to get ready their soup, and to rest themselves from their fatigues, when suddenly we got the order to march. The cooking-pots were emptied, and their forage taken from the horses, and we bridled up as quickly as possible. Again the enemy's cavalry had disturbed us. Up to this they had merely given us a foretaste of their power, and caused us to hasten our marches; it was now that they began to display themselves in all their vigour and dash.

The enemy, by their formidable attack, had thrust themselves between our *corps d'armee*, scattered along the frontier. They had already pierced the first line, and they now endeavoured to beat us in detail, and thus prevent the junction of the various parts. It was to their cavalry they entrusted the execution of this important duty. To attain this end, two regiments pushed on to Nancy. On their arrival at this place, they announced that all resistance was useless, as they were the advanced guard of a large army. This intelligence was conveyed to Lunéville, and again we made off, changing our line of retreat to the left by Colombey, Beaumont, Neufchateau, and Joinville.

It may well be asked, What was our cavalry doing all this time? Since the enemy that stopped our progress was so weak, why did we not send out parties to gain intelligence and overthrow them? Why did we not imitate their activity, instead of allowing them to oblige us to change our line of retreat as they pleased? Our cavalry had already shown their bravery at Froeschwiller; why not give them an opportunity of displaying their intelligence? They wished to be allowed to act, and grumbled at the inactivity to which they were condemned.

But instead of sending us out as far as possible, we were massed in divisions of five or six regiments together, and hampered with a baggage train; we never sent out a single scout or *vedette*, but were content to follow the main roads and simply accomplish the march. In short, it was a mere trial of speed, in which our only thought was to escape being cut off. Thus, it is evident that the part played by our cavalry in this long retreat, a part that might have been so important, was simply *nil*, as we neither obtained information nor fought.

From Joinville we marched towards Chalons, passing on our way by Vitry, and our line of retreat still depended on the extreme point reached by the enemy's cavalry, who pushed on their advanced parties to long distances to occupy the villages. As our route was continually being changed, the rations never came up until a late hour, and were then generally short in quantity. Moreover, owing to our bad habit of not quartering ourselves in the villages, we got but little rest. During the whole of the month of August it rained ceaselessly, and we had for camping-grounds fields under water. The earth was so soaked that our picketing-pegs had no hold; we had neither shelter nor straw to sleep on, and, owing to the heavy rain, we could neither light fires nor dry our clothes.

The horses were equally miserable. The wind blew away a portion of their scanty rations, and, pressing together, with their backs up and their heads out, they endeavoured to protect themselves against the weather. Every morning we had to march, and men and horses left the species of bog in which they were encamped, stiff, tired, and out of spirits. How much better our enemy understood the art of war! Aware of the extreme importance of preserving above all things the strength of their troops, they quartered them on the inhabitants. Immediately on their arrival, the men were housed and the horses put into barns; in this manner they rested and dried themselves, were well fed, and in the best condition to continue the struggle.

By our system of bivouacking we imagine that we lessen the cost of war for the inhabitants, but such is not the case, for soldiers who have to bivouac lay hands on all the wood and straw that can be found for cooking and camping purposes. It would be less expensive for a peasant to give a place at his fire, as he would then avoid waste. Besides all this, if you do away with tents, you lessen the amount carried by the horse, and could thus get more work out of him, as you would enable him to rest himself, by putting him under shelter every night.

On August 20th, the *corps d'armee* of Marshal MacMahon arrived at Chalons. We imagined that we should now receive reinforcements, in order to make up for our losses at Froeschwiller; but, in spite of the returns of the killed and wounded and the applications for reinforcements, we found no steps had been taken to assist us in this matter. Marshal MacMahon was now to take command of four *corps d'armee*, including a large cavalry force. The campaign is about to enter a fresh phase, but, before giving a description of it, we will discuss the part played by the cavalry in the battles fought round Metz.

PART 2

CHAPTER 1

Battle of Spicheren

After the unimportant success that General Frossard obtained at Sarrebruck on 2nd of August, he took up a position on the right of the Sarre, placing himself *a cheval* on the Forbach road, with his right resting on Spicheren, and his left in the direction of Stiring; his reserve was in the rear.

On the 6th of August, General Steinmetz ordered his cavalry to pass through Sarrebruck and gain the left bank of the Sarre. Following them up closely, he attacked our 2nd *corps d'armee*. After an obstinate and sanguinary engagement, the enemy stormed the wooded heights of Spicheren and Stiring, and General Frossard was obliged to retire on Forbach, and from there to St. Avoid.

Our cavalry who had had nothing to do during the day, found an opportunity of acting towards evening. As the troops who were entrusted with the duty of guarding the outlets from the woods had been forced to retire, there was no one left at this point but a company of engineers and a portion of the 12th Dragoons. Two squadrons of this regiment were accordingly dismounted, and, under cover of some slight earthworks hastily thrown up by the engineers, opened fire on the heads of the advancing columns.

Having succeeded in checking their advance, they remounted and charged the enemy, whom they repulsed. After this brilliant feat of arms, they retired behind the line of railway; and, with the assistance of the engineers, they maintained this position long enough to give the troops who occupied Forbach time to make the dispositions they wished. This episode in the battle deserves to be mentioned, as it concerns cavalry soldiers fighting on foot.

Chapter 2

Retreat to Metz

After this battle, the army fell back towards Metz, and between the 7th and 14th the cavalry did but little. In the course of this retreat, General de Cissey, commanding the 1st division of the 4th Corps, losing patience at the continual surveillance that the enemy's cavalry, according to their intelligent custom, exercised over him, ordered the 2nd Hussars to put a stop to it. A squadron of this regiment was accordingly told off to drive back the enemy. By his energetic attack, Captain Jouvenot, the officer in command of the squadron, drove in the Prussian outposts; but, having pursued too far, he was repulsed. Captain Jouvenot was killed, and several officers and men wounded in this affair; but from that time forth our army was allowed to retire unmolested to Metz.

In the course of the 10th, 11th, 12th, 13th, and 14th, various reconnaissances were made by the *Chasseurs d'Afrique*; of these, one example deserves mention. The German cavalry had entered the town of Pont-à-Mousson and cut the telegraph wires and the railway. Informed of what was going on, General de Margueritte turned out his brigade at 1:30 o'clock, proceeded as quickly as possible along the left bank of the Moselle, and arrived about 4 o'clock at Pont-à-Mousson. The 3rd squadron of the 1st Chasseurs d'Afrique, passing through some orchards, galloped up the railway and caught the Germans at work in the railway station.

The remainder of the brigade, sword in hand, charged, notwithstanding the slipperiness of the pavement, up the streets to the end of the town. There they were received with a fire from the windows. General de Margueritte, who was in the thick of the affair, was attacked by a Prussian officer, who aimed at his head; his forage cap, however, was alone cut, and the Prussian fell covered with wounds.

At the termination of some other reconnaissances that were pushed along the Moselle, the Prussian cavalry, consisting of four regiments, after exchanging shots, left the plateau of Mouzon, having sustained a loss of two officers and fourteen men killed, and two officers, thirty-two rank and file, forty-one horses, prisoners, who were brought into Metz.

On the 14th, the French Army was concentrated round Metz. and our forces, which, at the beginning of the war had been scattered along the frontier, now formed two distinct armies; namely, that of Marshal Bazaine and that of MacMahon. Both these armies had in view one object; namely, to unite beyond the forests of the Argonne, and the enemy's object was to prevent this junction. To attain this end, the Prussians executed a turning movement and set themselves to cross the Moselle to the south of Metz; their object being to retain and prevent Bazaine's retreat. The 1st Prussian Army, under the command of Steinmetz, tried to take us in flank; whilst the 2nd, under Prince Frederick Charles, was occupied in turning us by Pont-à-Mousson.

Attacked on the 14th at Borny, the French, in order to check the enemy, who, in spite of all his efforts, was unable to surround us, were obliged to suspend their march. But, as after this unsuccessful action we were obliged to fall back on Verdun, we wasted precious time on the 14th and 15th in the neighbourhood of Metz. As the line of retreat for the 2nd and 6th corps lay through Rézonville, Mars-la-Tour, and Mauheulles, General de Forton was ordered to reconnoitre for this column. His division consisted of the brigades Murat (1st and 9th Dragoons) and De Grammont (7th and 10th Cuirassiers).

On the evening of the 14th, General de Forton bivouacked on both sides of the Mars-la-Tour road, just beyond the post-house, and he had two troops of *cuirassiers* on outpost, one placed opposite the wood of Ognons and the other opposite the wood of Vaux; in addition there were two parties of dragoons placed in the direction of the wood of St. Arnould.

On the morning of the 15th, some peasants informed us of the presence of Prussian troops close to Ars, and they told us likewise that a large body of cavalry had been seen close to Novéant. The truth was, that Prince Frederick Charles had availed himself of his cavalry to make a reconnaissance on a large scale along the left bank of the Moselle. Their cavalry established contact with us on the 15th, and, according to their usual custom, they spread their nets to catch us as soon as we came up.

On the morning of the 15th, Forton's division set out to reconnoitre the Mars-la-Tour road in the direction that the enemy's *vedettes* had been seen. The brigade of dragoons led in order to search the ground round Tronville and Puxieux. Some troops of these, who were out feeling the way, were stopped at this village by the fire of the Prussian artillery. General Murat now sent to General de Forton for support, and the officer who carried the message was attacked as he returned by some of the enemy's lancers, who were concealed in a hollow.

General de Forton, passing by Mars-la-Tour, now brought up De Grammont's brigade and two batteries of artillery. He posted the artillery on the *plateau* looking towards Puxieux; behind it came the 7th Cuirassiers; at a distance of some 150 yards from the walls of Mars-la-Tour, and at about the same distance, but stretching beyond the village, came the 10th Cuirassiers. Whilst the artillery duel was progressing, in a fashion which did but little damage on either side, the enemy's skirmishers, taking advantage of a small ravine, boldly advanced to within 300 yards of us. Two troops advanced mounted against the enemy, and, assisted by the fire of a dismounted party, succeeded in forcing them to retire, and shortly after the artillery fire ceased.

Forton's division now proceeded to the camping-ground at Vionville and there encamped; the brigade of dragoons was placed at the foot of the ridge on the *plateau* near Vionville, and the *cuirassier* brigade on the opposite side of the road. But the general in command (De Grammont), considering that this position was bad, owing to its being in a hollow, and to the *cuirassiers* having no carbines to defend themselves in case of attack, ordered them to shift, and placed them close to De Valabrègue's division.

The division of General de Valabrègue had mounted on hearing the sound of the fight on this day, in order to support, if needful, but, finding it was unnecessary, had come back and taken up ground in rear of Vionville. During the night the dragoons and *cuirassiers* were protected by strong piquets. As for the enemy, still keeping their contact by means of their scouts, they; ascertained our smallest movements, and, as their object was, at all risks, to cut off our retreat, they marched the whole of the night of the 15th and 16th, and, having traversed an immense tract of ground, by morning they were ready to dispute the passage.

On the morning of the 16th the French Army occupied the following positions. The 2nd corps was in front of Rézonville, to the left of the Verdun road; the 6th at about the same distance on the right;

the 3rd was between Vernéville and St. Marcel; the 4th was marching to Doncourt; and the Guard occupied Gravelotte. The cavalry division of General de Forton was at Vionville, and that of General du Barail at Conflans.

CHAPTER 3

Battle of Rézonville, August 16th

General de Forton's cavalry had been ordered to march at 5 a. m., but this was countermanded, and at 9 the saddles and bridles were taken off. The dragoon officer in charge of the piquet had twice sent in to announce the approach of a large body of cavalry and artillery; a staff officer was sent out to see if this was the case; he returned and said there was nothing of importance going on, and the order to take the horses to water was accordingly issued, the arrangement being that whilst three squadrons per regiment were being watered, the fourth was to be on the lookout.

Scarcely had they arrived at the watering-place, when the Prussian artillery opened fire with a storm of shells, and both the bivouacs and villages were literally riddled. They had got information from their scouts of our carelessness, and had accordingly brought up their artillery at a gallop, and placed it on both sides of the road, from which position they fired as fast as they could.

Immediately there was a panic in the streets of Vionville. The men mounted their horses and pushed up the road, which was encumbered with wagons and loose horses. The officers, in spite of the heavy fire, tried to stop their men, but only succeeded with great difficulty; finally they managed to restore order in a few troops, and these served as a rallying-point to the remainder; they now returned to the *plateau* of Rézonville.

The *cuirassier* brigade, who, fortunately for themselves, had quitted their first ground and gone further to the rear, escaped this shower of shells; they now mounted in perfect order, and to avoid being cut off by large bodies of the enemy's cavalry, which threatened their right, they retired behind the wood which borders the Roman road on the east; then, passing in front of Villers aux Bois, they debouched on to

39

the *plateau* of Rézonville, a little to the right of the 9th Dragoons.

De Valabrègue's division, who had been on the *qui vive,* mounted quickly and arrived soon after, and in order to get under cover from the enemy's artillery, they also placed themselves close to the wood of Villers. This division was composed of General de Valabrègue's brigade (4th and 5th Chasseurs) and Bachelier's (7th and 12th Dragoons).

At the sound of the cannonade the 2nd corps stood to their arms and formed up; General Bataille's division was on the right, General Verge's on the left, and Lapasset's brigade refused and was extended to the right by Marshal Canrobert. Two attacks are now prepared against us: the front one from Mars-la-Tour and Thionville, the other on the left from the wood of Gorze. Up to about 11 o'clock the action was undecided, but at that moment General Bataille was wounded, and on the left of the 2nd corps we began to give ground. To put a stop to this and to re-establish the battle, General Frossard determined to charge the enemy's infantry, and accordingly ordered up the cavalry.

The 3rd Lancers formed the first line, and beyond them was General Desvaux's division, who had taken up a position on the right of the Rézonville road, in rear of that village, and at a distance of about 1,000 yards from our lines. General Desvaux now ordered General de Preuil to advance in support with the *cuirassiers* of the Guard along the other side of the road and in rear of the 3rd Lancers. This movement was immediately executed, and the regiment, placed parallel to the brow of the hill and a little below it, was under cover.

A few minutes afterwards this formation was changed to a double-column formation, with the fifth squadron in reserve. Towards 11:30 the fire, which had been very severe, slackened a moment, and suddenly we saw our skirmishers falling back in disorder over the brow of the hill. They were closely followed by the enemy's artillery, who crowned the heights and commenced to shell the cavalry. Two squadrons of the 3rd Lancers now advanced, but, as they received no order to charge, they came back after going a short way.

General de Preuil now sent to inform General Desvaux that in this part of the field there was a general retreat, and almost immediately he received the order to charge. This officer's command was at so great a distance from the enemy's infantry that the success of a charge was doubtful, unless preceded by a heavy artillery fire, which should make some impression on them. This objection was raised, but General Frossard himself came up and said, "Charge immediately, or we are all lost."

General de Preuil immediately ordered the first *échelon* to advance, and they galloped off in good order. The second followed at about 150 yards distance, but, as they were going too fast, the general ordered them to slacken their pace, and, accompanied by his staff, placed himself on the flank. In the meantime the first line, going as fast as they could, left the second a long way behind. As soon as the enemy's skirmishers saw our *cuirassiers* start, they formed rallying squares as quickly as possible, and in doing so had ceased firing.

The advance accordingly arrived at a good distance, and without much loss, when suddenly they were hindered by various obstacles which lay in their way. These consisted of biscuit barrels, baggage wagons, and) camp equipment that had been abandoned by the troops in their hurried retreat.

Obstructed in their advance, the 1st line inclined to its left, and the further they went, the greater the pressure became, and ended by throwing the two squadrons into disorder, so that when they received at thirty paces distance the terrible fire of the enemy, they were thrown into hopeless confusion and rushed forward into the intervals of the Prussian squares. The lieutenant-colonel was badly wounded; the commandant, although mortally wounded, nevertheless forced his way into a square, followed only by an adjutant, who was killed dead on the spot. As for the others, obliged, in order to retreat, to go right round the squares, they received the fire of all four faces, and were annihilated.

The 2nd line was now unmasked; they were received by a file fire, when at a distance of about 300 yards; this made a few gaps in the line, but they continued in good order, for the fire ceased for a moment; but when at 100 yards distance they got the order to charge, the enemy poured in such a hail of bullets that more than half the line was knocked over. The remainder got entangled in the obstacles that covered the ground, or else fell into a ditch that was dug about ten paces in front of the squares.

The 3rd line was equally unsuccessful, and was dispersed by the fire like the two preceding ones.

Whilst the *cuirassiers* of the guard tried to re-form, they were pursued by two regiments of Prussian cavalry, who passed through the intervals between the Prussian squares; one regiment came through the right centre interval; the other regiment (15th Lancers) came through the other interval, and were received with a sharp fire at a short distance from our skirmishers, who, not having had time to retire, had lain down in the ditches along the roadside. This fire stopped the pursuit of this regiment. As for the enemy's hussars, with the greatest daring, they pursued so far that they succeeded in surrounding the marshal.

The latter, as well as the whole of the staff, were obliged to draw swords and join in the *mêlée*, when a squadron of the 5th Hussars, and another of the 4th Chasseurs, warned in time by General de Preuil, arrived extremely apropos, and rescued the marshal and his staff. This charge of our hussars and *chasseurs* was made perpendicularly to the road, and presented our flank to the Prussian squares, who were, however, unable to fire, as their men were between us and them. Our *cuirassier* regiment lost in this charge 22 officers, 208 rank and file, and 243 horses.

As the squares that were charged remained unbroken, the result was almost nil. It is to be supposed that had the artillery opened fire on the line that was to be attacked, as General de Preuil desired, a different result might have been obtained.

Another conclusion that may be formed is, that the ground ought to have been previously reconnoitred, as, had that been done, the charge might have received a different direction.

At the same time that the enemy displayed his attack on Rézonville, the cavalry, under the command of Duke William of Mecklenburg,[1] endeavoured to overthrow our 6th Corps, and some batteries of artillery who had been pushed on ahead on the *plateau*, with a battalion of *chasseurs* as an escort. The enemy began by crushing our fire with a superior one; he then sent forward two lines of cavalry in *échelon* at a distance of about 100 yards from each other; the first line was composed of *cuirassiers* and the second of lancers. These two lines charged, overthrew the *chasseurs à pied*, in spite of their well-sustained fire, sabered our batteries as they passed, and endeavoured to annihilate the remnants of our foot soldiers. But they were unaware that the moment of reckoning had arrived, and that they were about to be cut in pieces by our cavalry.

We have already related how de Forton's and Valabrègue's divisions at the termination of certain movements had gone and placed themselves near the wood which borders the Roman road. On arrival, the two brigades of General de Forton were formed in column of regiments, right in front, and had executed several changes of front, sometimes with a view to facing Rézonville and sometimes Vionville. The

---

1. The cavalry here referred to was under the command of Gen. von Rheinbaben. Duke William commanded another cavalry division.—A. L. W.

last time this movement took place, they became inverted not only in each regiment, but in each squadron, and in this formation proceeded to the top of the *plateau*, keeping the wood close to the Roman road in their rear.

On seeing the enemy's cavalry amongst our batteries. General de Forton ordered the dragoons and a portion of the *cuirassiers* to advance. They deployed and attacked the advancing lines. In the charge the 9th Dragoons passed through the Prussian *cuirassiers*, who opened their ranks, without stopping, and inclined to the right and left against our artillery, and then pushed on to rejoin the lancers. Their charge terminated, the lancers wheeled about to retire, but were attacked by our *cuirassiers*, who charged to the command, "*Cuirassiers*, attention; go!" As these words indicate no sort of formation, they advanced in a confused mass, the officers being forced to push their horses to the utmost in order to keep ahead of the men, who were riding with their reins completely loose.

A terrible *mêlée* now took place; the 16th Prussian Lancers, taken in flank, were overthrown, sabered, and actively pursued, when suddenly the white *cuirassiers* came up to their assistance. Their horses, however, were so blown with their long advance that they were thoroughly done. It was now our turn, and the cavalry of General de Valabrègue advanced to join de Forton's, and engaged the enemy. The fight was now at its height, and was waged with the greatest fury on both sides. The eagerness of our men was so great, and the two sides were so mixed up, that, in spite of the trumpets sounding the rally, the massacre went on.

In a few seconds the enemy's cavalry was annihilated and the ground strewn with the dead bodies of lancers and white *cuirassiers*. The best mounted and those taken prisoners alone escaped. At this moment the infantry from the side of Vionville opened fire on the ground on which the 7th Cuirassiers were operating. The retreat was therefore sounded and our regiments were re-formed and proceeded to Gravelotte.

This affair was exceedingly creditable to us, and our losses, compared to those of our enemy, were insignificant, and the way to account for this is that we use the point of our swords, and thus manage to get between the joints of the *cuirass* and the portion of the helmet that covers the back of the neck, whilst they, on the other hand, make cuts and fire off their pistols, thus only wounding the horses, as most of the men were protected by their *cuirasses*.

The German account of this business being a slight stretch of the imagination, we will also give it.

With respect to the "Death Charge" that General von Bredow's cavalry made against two batteries of artillery .and some infantry, the Count de Schmetow, a major of *cuirassiers*, who himself had two bullets put through his helmet, gives the following account:

It was an inexcusable thing for a commander to lead his troops to certain death, unless obliged to do so for important reasons; this was, however, the case.

Colonel Voigts-Rhetz, the chief of the staff of the 3rd Army Corps came to General von Bredow, commanding our brigade, and who is in the habit of always commanding us, and said to him: 'The general commanding and General von Rheinbaben, commanding the cavalry division, are agreed that it is your business to charge along the wood, and still you remain here.' To this General von Bredow answered: 'Do you mean to say that I ought to overthrow that infantry along the wood?'

'Certainly,' was the answer; 'we have already taken the village, and, as we were not able to advance against the wood, the fate of the battle depends on this, that you sweep away everything along the wood, and you must attack with the greatest vigour.' Two lines were accordingly formed in *échelon*: the *cuirassiers* on the left along the edge of the wood, and the lancers on the right, about 100 yards in rear. Our brave general charged with four officers of his staff, three of whom were killed. We scarcely gave the first battery time to fire two of its pieces when we were already on them. It seemed to me that the object in this death ride of ours was not so much to obtain trophies as to sweep away everything between the wood and the road. In the battery, we killed every one, and then gave chase to a column of infantry, whom we rode over; nevertheless, they sent some shots after us when we had passed.

Cuirassiers and lancers now formed together. We attacked a second battery, and all who did not run away were ridden over, and in company with the runaways we came up to a second column of infantry. Just before we got up to them, some squadrons of French *cuirassiers* came out from an opening in the wood, and after we had ridden over this second column of infantry, our small body of men was mixed up pell-mell with the French *cuirassiers*; the lancers were on our right.

We now retreated, and I shall never forget the way we did so, from the point where our charge, a charge of a quarter of a German mile in length, terminated. I ordered the first trumpeter I could find to sound the regimental call. The trumpet, which had been pierced with bullets, gave out such an unearthly sound as went through my very bones.

On the roll being called, out of eleven platoons (three were detached) we could only get together three. The regiment had lost 7 officers and 200 men.

A short time after the charges we have described took place, Gen. de Ladmirault, who commanded our right wing, and who had marched to the sound of the cannon, found himself opposed by the enemy in considerable force. The divisions of the 4th corps, who had advanced with success as far as the *plateau* of Gréyère, were now stopped by the enemy's infantry, preceded by artillery, debouching by Mars-la-Tour; they were also threatened in flank by a large body of cavalry.

This body of cavalry was composed as follows: The brigade of dragoons of the Guard, Barby's brigade, two other regiments, von Rheinbaben's division (4th Cuirassiers, 17th and 19th Dragoons, 13th Lancers, 10th Hussars), and the 16th Dragoons belonging to the Vraatz infantry division. From his position at the farm of Gréyère, General de Ladmirault examined the field of battle. A ravine and deep stream were at his feet, and on the opposite side were the fields lying between Mars-la-Tour and Jarny, and which border the road that connects these two places. The whole of this ground has a gentle slope to the N.W., and about half way down is a sudden dip. The general crossed the ravine, taking with him a battery of 12-pounders,[3] which, by its fire, kept off two regiments of dragoons who were advancing.

Immediately guessing what the enemy were after, the commander of the 4th corps ordered the 5th battalion of *chasseurs à pied* of Grenier's division to advance, and placed the 98th regiment in rear in a wood; he then collected as large a force of cavalry as possible to protect his menaced flank. The regiments that composed this force and their disposition was as follows: In rear of the right, and at about 500 yards from the farm of Gréyère, were the 2nd Chasseurs d'Afrique under General du Barail. Next to them came the 2nd and 7th Hussars and 3rd Dragoons, under the command of General Legrand. (The 11th Dragoons, who likewise were under this officer, were in rear of the infantry.)

3. French.

45

At the same distance as the village of Bruville were the dragoons and lancers of the Guard, under General de France. Lastly, De Clérembault's division of the 3rd Army Corps was near the village of Bruville; this division consisted of the 2nd, 3rd, and 10th Chasseurs and the 2nd, 4th, 5th, and 8th Dragoons. (The regiments of *chasseurs* were not complete, owing to their having detached portions of them with the infantry, and the 5th and 8th Dragoons were just at this moment with the Marshal commanding the 3rd Army Corps.)

Thus on both sides large masses of cavalry are about to come on the scene, and afford a grand though terrible sight. About 4:30 p. m., whilst our troops were engaged in front, one of the enemy's batteries was detached to take us in flank, and with that object took up a position on the road itself, nearly in a line with the Gréyère Farm; in order to avoid being turned it was absolutely necessary to silence this fire; accordingly General de Ladmirault gave Generals du Barail, Legrand, and de France the order to employ the cavalry to protect his right. Immediately General du Barail passed over the ravine that lay in his front, with the 2nd Chasseurs d'Afrique, wheeled to the left, and charged the battery in skirmishing order.

The enemy had scarcely time to fire before our men were on them. The 2nd sabered the gunners as they fled, and, still continuing their advance, they came in contact with a superior force of the enemy; they managed, however, to disengage themselves by going off to the right; and, rallying in the angle formed by the wood and the road, they opened a sharp fire on the enemy. After this brilliant feat of arms, the battery was no more seen.

In the meanwhile, Generals Legrand and de France had made their arrangements for attacking the advancing German cavalry, who were in a formation resembling a pair of tongs.

The first of these masses was on a line perpendicular to the road, with its right about 200 yards from it; the second mass was formed in two lines almost parallel to the road.

Legrand's division, which was in line, went troops "right wheel," crossed the ravine and road, and then formed line to the front perpendicularly to the road. The 3rd Dragoons remained in reserve on the right. De France's brigade (lancers and dragoons of the Guard), with the lancers in front, passed the ravine in the same formation as the 1st brigade and further to the right; they then went in the direction of the southern edge of wood by the Gréyère farmhouse and formed line to the left at a trot.

In this manner our hussar brigade was opposed to the 1st body of the enemy, and our brigade of Guards, including the 3rd Dragoons, to the 2nd body. General Legrand now got a second time the command to attack at once, from the general commanding. General du Barail, who was there, however, observed it was too late, and the right moment had passed. At the same time, as the distance was great, one of the colonels of the hussars asked permission to open fire on the enemy, who had halted on the sky-line. General Legrand, however, anxious to attack the enemy, and only taking counsel from his own courage, answered: "No; draw swords," and immediately ordered General de Montaigu's brigade to advance.

The German dragoons, motionless on the crest and coming out against the sky-line like giants, at first waited for us; then, when our hussars were quite close, they fired their carbines, which are attached to the saddle, and, drawing swords, they advanced with a loud cheer and in good order. These dragoons formed the right of the formation that has been already likened to a pair of tongs.

The shock was terrible. The majority of our horses, small and blown by the distance they had advanced over, were, as it were, broken against the species of wall that the enemy's line presented, in addition to which their horses were much bigger. The 7th Hussars charged through an interval onto a regiment in close column. They then endeavoured to return and take part in the fight, which now became severe; amongst others, General de Montaigu was wounded and taken prisoner.

General Legrand, with a bravery that deserves to be recorded, charged a hundred yards in front of the dragoons that he was bringing up in support of his 1st line. He attacked a regiment of the enemy's dragoons, who gave way before our onslaught, and, covered with wounds, fell at the head of the regiments he had led so bravely.

This first seething mass of combatants was now increased by more regiments coming and falling one over the other.

General de France, finding himself attacked on the flank, hurriedly sent the lancers, who had barely time to form, to the front. The left of this regiment came in contact with the right of Legrand's brigade; their centre broke through the German dragoons, and their right came against the Prussian lancers, who took them in flank and knocked them over. Then our dragoons of the Guard, who also had scarcely had time to form, pushed to the rescue of our lancers, fell on the enemy's lancers, and annihilated them. Finally, to complete the chaos, on the Prussian side up came hussars and *cuirassiers*, and on ours the *chasseurs d'Afrique*. Confusion was then at its height.

It was then neither an attack nor an ordinary fight, but a kind of furious *mêlée* or whirlpool in which 6,000 cavalry soldiers, dressed in all sorts of uniforms, armed in every conceivable manner, were killing each other as fast as they could, some with the point of the sword, others with the forte.

Our unfortunate lancers were taken, on account of their blue revers, for Prussian dragoons, and were accordingly slain without mercy. In the midst of pistol shots and the sound of swords clashing one against another, one could hear cries of "Don't attack us; we are French!"

"No quarter!" was the only answer from our dragoons, who went on killing, thinking that it was a ruse on the part of the enemy. Here, indeed, were enacted some terrible scenes; but how was one to put a stop to them? Seeing this dreadful *mêlée'*, General de France ordered the recall to be sounded, and our men returned in disorder, and were re-formed about the place from which the attacks had commenced.

At first the enemy's cavalry followed us, but, recalled by their own trumpets, they remounted the brow of the hill, and we proceeded with our formation, protected on the left by the fire of the *chasseurs d'Afrique* and two companies of the 5th Chasseurs à Pied that General Grenier had posted behind the trees on the Verdun road, and on the right by some men who had been dismounted at the edge of the wood, by the 5th Chasseurs à Pied, who had come up from Gréyère, and also by the 98th regiment, which was in the wood that lies between the Verdun road and Gréyère farm; finally, by the fire of the 12-pounders that General de Ladmirault had brought up to support the attack.

Our infantry fire almost annihilated a regiment of Prussian dragoons of the Guard, who tried to surprise us by coming round the head of the ravine. The 2nd regiment of the same brigade met a similar fate a little further off, and lost even their guidon, in trying to aid a Prussian column that was in a critical position. After the fight we have just described, the enemy's cavalry had at first again taken up their old position on the brow of the hill, but they afterwards retreated, owing to the arrival of General de Clérembault. This officer was not informed of the action the cavalry was about to take, but, perceiving from the place where he was, the dust raised up by Legrand's charge, he advanced as quickly as possible, in order to join in the fray and render success certain. The regiments of chasseurs who formed his right descended into the ravine so as to join in the *mêlée*, but, being too far to the right, they were met by the retreating hussars, and some disorder was the result of the meeting.

General de Clérembault now crossed the ravine with the 4th Dragoons, and, as soon as he reached the plateau, charged. They sabered some of the last of the retreating enemy, and the Prussians now finally retired towards Mars-la-Tour. Thus ended this sanguinary conflict, at the end of which we remained masters of the field. It would be necessary to go very far back in history before one could come upon a cavalry engagement in which such large masses had charged each other. The number of killed and wounded was considerable, but our object was attained, as the enemy had to desist from trying to turn our right.

A final charge terminated this series of engagements. After darkness had set in, the Prussians retired, when suddenly on our left the sound of cavalry at a gallop was heard approaching. A regiment of red hussars passed through our infantry, but the *zouaves*, as soon as they had recovered from their surprise, took post in the ditches along the roadside and dispersed this party, who could scarcely be distinguished, and whose attack seemed to be without any definite object.

CHAPTER 4

Observations on the Employment of the Cavalry at Rézonville

How many lessons we may learn from the engagements that we have just described! Never in any battle was cavalry so desperately employed. On this long day (16th), on which we fought for upwards of ten hours, we had seen the effect of this arm under numberless circumstances. It was by the help of his cavalry that the enemy was enabled at the commencement of the battle to compensate for a numerical inferiority by making its repeated charges replace the troops he was in need of, and thus, by causing delay, give time for reinforcements to come up.

We will not now enter upon the part played by the cavalry, from a strategic point of view, as we will discuss that later on. But from the examples that have been already given we can deduce tactical truths which illustrate the following observations:

On the part of the enemy, as well as on our own, charges were begun at absurd distances. In addition, starting at too rapid a pace at first, the horses, used up by having, to gallop 1,000, 1,500, and even 2,000 yards, were completely blown on arriving at the wished-for point, and were therefore inc pable of insuring success. Amongst other instances, we will quote the charge of von Bredow's brigade. When it was taken in flank by our cavalry, the horses were so done up that the men could do nothing with them, and they were accordingly at the mercy of our soldiers, who broke through them, knocking them over and scattering them like sheep.

This same charge likewise proves the necessity of a reserve, which should support the movement without hurry, and should arrive on the scene quite fresh, in order to take advantage of the enemy's being tired and blown. Von Bredow's brigade was at first successful, but, as it had no support, they were unable to preserve their success, and finally they were entirely at our mercy.

If we look at the charges that were made against infantry, we shall see that they failed because it had not first been shaken by a cannonade. This truth is so old that it seems almost foolish to repeat it. Nevertheless, this error was over and over again committed, and always with one same result; namely, the useless destruction of the troops who were engaged. Take, for example, the gallant charge of our *cuirassiers* of the Guard. Besides, in this case we had neglected to send out squadron *vedettes*, and, consequently, before reaching the goal they arrived at, the line was broken up by the obstacles it encountered on its path.

As for two bodies of cavalry meeting in full swing, this happened repeatedly; and, in contradiction of the old belief, that one of the two half-turns before the final shock. We must, therefore, for the future study the causes that lead both to success and to the reverse. The horses of our light cavalry were knocked to pieces against the solid and impassable line formed by the German dragoons. From this it appears that as the advantage is on the side of size and weight, one should never engage when there is too great a disparity, but have for this reason cavalry of various sorts in each brigade.

We must also point out that many of our regiments were surprised and attacked whilst in the middle of a formation, and that they were obliged to charge before finishing the movement, thus bringing about confusion and taking away the men's presence of mind and coolness; to this may be attributed the fact of our lancers having been mistaken for Prussians by our dragoons, and attacked as such.

All this proves how necessary it is to avoid on the field of battle a succession of movements! before one can face the enemy, and for this reason in peace-time we should only practice a few rapid and simple movements, which should do away with all hesitation as to which of them one is to choose. Lastly, we may remark that one reason why we did not obtain a more decisive success was that the regiments engaged were directed by a divided authority. Three generals had a separate command to attain the same end; each attacked in the formation he preferred, and each sounded the recall when he thought fit.

How is it then possible to obtain a certain success if each has the power of interfering with the plan of his neighbour? This is precisely what happened in this charge. The recall that was sounded for only a portion of the troops engaged was mistaken for a general recall, and the whole of our men returned. We will now sum up the mistakes that were committed:

Charges begun too far off; no squadron *vedettes* sent out; unbroken infantry attacked; regiments surprised whilst forming; attacks entered upon without supports; the danger of opposing light cavalry to heavy; want of unity in the general command, there being no general-in-chief for the cavalry.

Such are the lessons that may be learnt by a study of the battle of Rézonville.

CHAPTER 5

Battle of Gravelotte, August 18th

At the conclusion of the battle fought on the 16th, the southern road leading to Verdun fell into the hands of the Prussians; the northern road, however, passing by St. Marie and the forest of Jaumont, was still open to us. In place of hastening his march, Marshal Bazaine remained in camp, at Metz, where he was about to be hemmed in by the Prussians. During the 17th, the enemy, by means of their cavalry, maintained their contact with us and prepared themselves for a general action on the 18th. At this battle the part played by our cavalry was unimportant. Along nearly the whole of our front the country was wooded, and on this account our army was on the defensive. This situation rendered difficult the employment of the cavalry, and the greater part of this arm remained massed during the battle in the grounds of Lessy, Chatel St. Germain, Moulin Longeau, and in rear of Amanvillers.

One may, however, record one instance of its utility on the right wing of our army, in the action fought by the 6th corps between St. Privat and Roncourt. At the time (*viz.*, about 6 p. m.) that the Prussians were trying to turn us by the village of Roncourt, Du Barail's division, which was formed up between St. Privat and Roncourt, made a movement so as to extend our right, and by this demonstration succeeded in holding the enemy in check for some time. The 4th corps sent General du Barail its brigade of dragoons (2nd and 11th), and these took part in the operations. The 3rd Chasseurs were ordered to charge, and were led by General de Brichard. The regiment advanced in column, and came across a wall behind which some of the enemy's infantry was concealed.

On our approach they opened a remarkably well sustained fire, which, however, did not do our men much damage, as they aimed too low, but caused a great loss of horses. Some of the *chasseurs* jumped the wall and were taken prisoners, but the majority fell back without having engaged the enemy, who were too well sheltered behind their rampart.

After the Battle of Gravelotte, the army of Marshal Bazaine was completely shut up in Metz. The various cavalry divisions bivouacked close to their army corps, and up to the 31st they were employed in repairing the disorder caused by the fighting and marches of the preceding few days. Several times the cavalry stood to their horses ready to march, but as a rule they did not mount.

CHAPTER 6

Attack on the Lines of St. Barbe

On the 31st August and 1st September, each cavalry division at first marched with its own army corps, which arrangement allowed the divisions attached to the 4th and 6th army corps to throw out for a short time, on arriving on the field of battle, a few squadrons to the front. But the enemy's infantry did not delay us long, and the cavalry had to go to the rear. Consequently, this enormous mass of cavalry, consisting of the divisions Desvaux (the guard), de Forton (the reserve), de Gondecourt (4th corps), were concentrated on the *plateau* to the east of Fort St. Julien, and on the other side of the road was du Barail's division (6th corps).

These divisions, as at the battle of Amanvillers, found that they were in such a position as precluded the possibility of moving, and in the event of a reverse they would have been destroyed by the enemy's shells.

On this occasion (31st) General de Clérembault's division had an opportunity of acting to a certain extent. About 4 p. m. it was ordered to proceed to the right of the 3rd corps and conform to the movements of the infantry. The division, by brigades in two lines, advanced to the front, covered by skirmishers, but, as the ground was unfavourable, they were obliged to form open column, and eventually advance by fours, which caused some confusion.

As General de Clérembault had been warned to support the movements of General Montaudon in turning the enemy's position, he advanced along the vineyards of Coincy and re-formed his division in open column, with the 5th Dragoons in front. Scarcely had the division reached the brow of the hill, when it came under a fire from Servigny, from a position some distance off on the left. The general now ordered his division, in order to get it under cover, to cross the ravine of Coincy, and formed it up in two lines on the opposite bank, just below 7 the slope opposite the village. On his left was the ravine of Coincy and Les Vines; on the right a piece of rising ground, behind which was the enemy's infantry. In front was a village surrounded by gardens, and occupied by the enemy's infantry, and in rear the wood which ended in the ravine of Colombey.

General de Clérembault, finding himself separated from the infantry, dismounted a squadron of the 5th Dragoons, and ordered them to leave their helmets fastened to their saddles, so that they might not be seen so easily, and to advance to the brow of the hill, and, as soon as they had got there, to lie down and return the enemy's fire. This movement was rapidly and successfully carried out, and at the same time a troop was sent to explore the wood of Colombey, where there was a good deal of firing going on. As our infantry did not come up, and as the fire from the village of Coincy augmented, our position became intolerable, and the general ordered the remainder of the 5th Dragoons to dismount and attack the village.

This order led to some confusion, and, as there was no time to lose, the 4th Dragoons, who were on the left of the 5th, received the order to carry out this operation. As soon as the dragoons had dismounted, they advanced at a double on Coincy firing as they went, and forced an entrance. The evening was coming on, and the enemy, imagining that they were attacked by a considerable force, offered but little opposition, and retired, taking advantage of the gardens that lay in rear of and to the right of the village, and keeping up a sharp fusillade. The 5th Dragoons now got the order to turn the village, and, taking the enemy in the rear, to charge.

Two squadrons moved to the front, but were unable to act, owing to the hedges and gardens. In spite of the fire opened on them, the regiments who remained mounted held their ground until the infantry, who were to occupy the village, came up. As night had now come on, the recall was sounded for the dragoons, and this cavalry division encamped close to the village of Montoy.

This is the second instance, in this campaign, of dragoons dismounting to attack and defend positions.

In the fighting that took place on the 1st September, the cavalry was not called upon to act. Towards noon the marshal intended, it is believed, to employ the cavalry, who were massed close to the Fort of St. Julien, and to make them charge along the *plateau* which lies between the village of Mey and the Bouzonville road, had the enemy attempted to pursue our infantry.

The chief command in this operation was entrusted to General Desvaux, who communicated to each commanding officer the part he was to take. Moreover, the ground was examined, but, as the enemy did not commit the mistake of following us up, no charge took place, and the regiments the same evening encamped on their old ground. Dating from the 1st September, the blockade of Metz was complete, and the *rôle* of the cavalry became naturally unimportant. Nevertheless, a system of scouting was organized in the 3rd and 4th corps, and the men who were selected for this duty acquitted themselves with intelligence. In addition to this, the various regiments foraged and made reconnaissances, but, with the exception of a few skirmishes, the history of the cavalry during this fatal period was insignificant.

During the long days that intervened before the capitulation, our sufferings increased day by day, and little by little the cavalry melted away.

On the 9th September, provisions had already begun to run short, and we had to furnish 1,000 horses to aid in feeding the troops. Soon this amount had to be increased, and we were barely able to feed those that were left. The men gathered up leaves wherever they could, to feed the horses, and did not hesitate to lead them out to graze even under the enemy's fire.

By the 21st the rations had been so cut down that more horses died than the commissariat wanted. Those that remained ate each other's manes and tails, dirt, or leaves. Every effort was made to keep them alive, not for combatant purposes, as they were so weak that they were unable to move, but in order to feed the army. We were able, at this time, to muster two squadrons a regiment, counting those horses which were still living, and the dismounted men were armed with chassepots and drilled to work as infantry.

Soon the mortality caused by famine became dreadful; it rained without ceasing, the whole camp was a sea of mud, and the ground was covered with such a number of dead horses that no one took the trouble to bury them. Those horses that were still standing in the lines were knocked up and quivering in every limb, without strength sufficient to swallow the leaves that stuck to their wasted lips, and, as soon as they fell to the ground, were torn to pieces by the famished soldiery. In spite of all our sufferings, the *morale* of the men did not diminish. Nearly always wet through, without shelter, food, or a change of clothes, they underwent the dreadful miseries of the last few days without a murmur, thus giving proof of their indomitable courage under reverses.

Thus vanished this numerous cavalry that we have pictured so brilliant as regards courage on the battlefield. Better for it had it perished altogether on the field where it had fought so well. At least it would not have survived to undergo a degradation worse than death itself–*viz*., capitulation. The bitter remembrance of this surrender will never be effaced from those who were unhappy enough to take part in it.

PART 3

CHAPTER 1

Army of Chalons

We left Marshal MacMahon, on August 20th, at the camp of Chalons, about to take command of the 1st, 5th, 7th, and 12th corps. As these corps were composed of anything but satisfactory materials, the Marshal intended to give them time to get themselves in order, and in a council, of which the Emperor was president, it was decided to retire on Paris. Seven divisions of cavalry were attached to this army. Five belonged to the different corps and two were in reserve. The cavalry of the different corps was as under:

1st corps, General Duhesme, three brigades: De Septeuil (3rd Hussars, 11th Chasseurs); De Nansouty (10th Dragoons, 2nd and 6th Lancers); Michel (8th and 9th Cuirassiers).

5th corps, General Brahaut, two brigades: De Bernis (5th Hussars, 12th Chasseurs); De la Mortière (3rd and 5th Lancers); the 3rd Lancers remained at Metz with Lapasset's brigade.

7th corps, General Ameil, two brigades: Cambriel (4th Hussars, 4th and 8th Lancers); Du Colombier (6th Hussars and 6th Dragoons); this brigade never joined.

12th corps, General Fénélon; this division belonged to the 6th corps at Metz, but never joined; two brigades: Savaresse (1st and 7th Lancers); Tillard (1st Hussars, 6th Chasseurs).

Another division, under the command of General Lichtlin, joined the 12th corps, at Rethel, on the 25th, and consisted of two brigades: De Beville (5th and 6th Cuirassiers); Néant (7th and 8th Chasseurs).

The two reserve divisions were composed as follows, *viz.*: 1st division (1st, 2nd, 3rd, and 4th Cuirassiers), under the command of General de Bonnemain; the 2nd under the command of General de Margueritte, consisted of the two regiments of *Chasseurs d'Afrique* who had come from Metz as an escort to the Emperor; also the 4th Chasseurs d'Afrique, who had just disembarked, and Tillard's brigade, which was withdrawn from General Fénélon's division.

CHAPTER 2

To Rheims, and from Rheims to Sedan

At 5 a. m. on the 21st, the army commenced its march to Rheims. The marshal started about 11 o'clock, and at midday the emperor, accompanied by his household, started in a carriage. A division of cavalry was left behind to cover the retreat and burn the camp at Chalons.

But at Paris they took alarm at this retrograde movement, and M. Rouher came to Rheims to discuss the plan of the campaign, and to endeavour to make the wishes of the Regency prevail. A council was called, the original plan abandoned, and Marshal MacMahon agreed to march to the rescue of the Metz army.

In order to fully comprehend the difficulties we had now to contend against, it is necessary to understand the enemy's position, and the forces with which he intended to oppose us.

One army, under the command of Prince Frederic Charles, blockaded Metz. Two other armies were marching on Paris. The one, under the command of the Crown Prince of Saxony, was advancing by Verdun; the other, under the Crown Prince of Prussia, had its route by Nancy and St. Dizier, and its cavalry was well ahead at Vitry-le-Français and Troyes.

The plan of campaign that Marshal MacMahon had adopted was therefore an extremely difficult one to carry out with success, as, in the first place, it was necessary to outstrip these two armies, and in addition, once adopted, it ought to have been acted upon with the greatest celerity, for the chance of success lay principally in taking the enemy by surprise. The large body of cavalry which Marshal MacMahon. had at his disposal would facilitate such an operation, almost hide it altogether by interposing itself like a curtain between our army and the enemy, and thus leave them hesitating in the plains of Champagne; only, in order to do this, it was necessary to unite it under the command of a skilful leader.

Such was the part we might have played, but if we look and see what we really did do and how we were employed, we shall find the cavalry generally marching either in unwieldy masses or else reconnoitring the opposite flank to that where the enemy was; always full of dash when called upon to charge, always wanting when called upon to reconnoitre and establish contact with the enemy. From the 20th to the 23rd General de Fénélon was ordered to reconnoitre, with the 1st and 4th Lancers and the 4th Chasseurs d'Afrique, the whole of the country that lies between the roads leading from Chalons to Vitry and from Chalons to St. Menehould. On the 23rd this division rejoined the 12th corps, and it is from this date that the distribution of the cavalry corresponds to the list already given.

On the 22nd the troops were warned that on the morrow they were to march in the direction of Montmédy, and accordingly on the 23rd they left Rheims for Bethniville. We now find them, after having wasted three days, returning to exactly the spot that they occupied on the evening of the 20th. The 7th corps (General Douai) was on the extreme right, and the 12th (General Lebrun) on the extreme left. The army had for the advance guard the two reserve cavalry divisions. General de Bonnemain's division was at Suippe and Vaudesincourt to protect the right, and General de Margueritte's, still farther in advance, went as far as Monthois, and was entrusted with the duty of observing the defiles of Argonne, Grandpré, and Croix-aux-Bois. The other cavalry regiments marched with their corps.

Scarcely had we started, when the marshal began to fear that he might run short of supplies, and accordingly directed his left on Rethel, which place he reached on the 24th.

General de Margueritte received the order to remain in observation at Monthois, and De Bonnemain's division was ordered to Pont Faverjet.

We had made good progress these first two days, and, by keeping it up, we might distance the enemy and arrive before Metz in four days. In place of doing so, however, we halted at Rethel.

The Crown Prince, informed by his cavalry of the change in our plans, immediately stopped in his advance on Paris, changed front, and proceeded northeast, following the line of the Meuse so as to threaten our right flank. On this side, therefore, lay our danger, and it was indispensable that it should be protected by cavalry. Instead, however, of taking this precaution, General de Bonnemain's division was sent to Rethel—*viz.*, to our left flank the opposite side to the enemy; and, in addition to this, General de Margueritte's division, which was now alone on the right flank, was sent to Semuy with orders to reconnoitre as far as possible, especially in the direction of Chêne Populeux. One battery of horse artillery of the 12th corps was ordered to proceed to Stenay and place itself at the disposal of General de Margueritte.

In consequence of these movements, General Douai (7th corps) found, on reaching Vouziers, that our cavalry had quitted the defiles of Grandpré and Croix-aux-Bois, and, therefore, that our right rear was completely unprotected. Unwilling to remain in such a position, he sent the 4th Hussars to Grandpré to ascertain, at all risks, the enemy's movements.

The Germans employed their cavalry in a very different fashion, and pushed on their scouts to enormous distances ahead. Those who preceded the army coming from Stenay were twenty-four miles in advance, and were to be met with beyond the defiles of the Argonne. On our arrival they fell back slowly, and only when they had ascertained our force, etc., and which information they reported. The Crown Prince's army, who were advancing by forced marches, acted in the same manner, throwing out their cavalry as a curtain behind which they could operate; they came rapidly up to us and began to threaten the 4th Hussars, who, as we have already remarked, had been sent to Grandpré to watch the enemy. This regiment having sent word to say that it had a stronger body of the enemy opposed to it than it could hold in check, General Douai came and took up a position a little in advance of Longwy. This movement kept the enemy back, and they confined themselves to some desultory skirmishes with the 4th Hussars.

On the 27th General de Margueritte's division was sent to watch the roads in the direction of Stenay and Dun, and their doing so rendered the passage of the Meuse at Mouzon and Remilly possible. On arriving at Chene Populeux, the marshal learnt of the arrival of the Saxons and the Crown Prince of Prussia, and, seeing that his march on Montmédy was compromised, he determined to move westward, and issued orders to that effect to the army.

During the night, however, the Minister of War telegraphed the following message:

Minister of War to MacMahon. The Council of Regency and

the Council of Ministers entreat you to succour Bazaine's Army, and unless you do so, a revolution in Paris is imminent.

Marshal MacMahon, with fatal results for France, again submits to a decision from Paris, resumes his march in the direction of Metz, and proceeds to Stenay.

Several roads lead from Chêne Populeux to Stenay: one, inclining to the south, passes by Harricourt, Bar, Buzancy, Nouart, and Stenay; another by Stône, where it branches off to Stenay, either by Beaumont and this is the most direct or else passing further north, by Roncourt, Mouzon, and Carignan. On the 28th the movement of the troops commenced, and the headquarters arrived at Stône. General de Margueritte's division went from Stône to Mouzon, close to the 5th corps (General de Failly), and General de Bonnemain's was at Petites-Armoises, a little in rear of the right.

On the 29th General de Bonnemain's division halted at Roncourt, and General de Margueritte's reconnoitred the right bank of the Meuse, in the direction of Stenay and Montmédy. The army corps marched very far apart. Those of Ducrot and Lebrun marched towards Mouzon and Carignan, and those of Douai and De Failly advanced by Harricourt and Buzancy.

The further we advanced, the more frequently we encountered the enemy's cavalry. At first *vedettes* and small parties of five or six continually appearing and disappearing, but always out of reach. Their duty was not to fight, but to watch continually, and this *rôle* they carried out to perfection all through the campaign.

CHAPTER 3

Battle of Buzancy

On arriving at Harricourt, General de Failly halted to concentrate his force, and he learnt that on the previous evening the Prussians had been requisitioning provisions there, and at that very moment they were at Buzancy. He sent on two squadrons of the 12th Chasseurs to reconnoitre, and these were received, on debouching into the plain, by a fire from two batteries posted on the hill that commands Buzancy and the Nouart road. Without pausing, our *chasseurs* mounted the hill, and, in spite of the heavy fire, charged the batteries in skirmishing order. They were still some 300 yards off, when two regiments of Saxon dragoons came out of the wood on the left of the road and advanced to support their guns.

The *chasseurs* now halted, fired, and recommenced their advance. In spite of their small numbers, they attack the Saxons sword in hand, our men using the point and the enemy cutting. Captain d'Ollonne was badly wounded on the head, and as our men could not hold their own for any time against such superior numbers, and as they were not supported by the lancer brigade in rear, they were compelled to fall back, which they did, again having recourse to their carbines.

On the morrow, hearing that the enemy were in considerable force on the high ground at Nouart, the chief of the staff of the 5th corps made a reconnaissance with the cavalry and a battery of artillery. But this was carried out without either an advanced guard or flankers, and consequently we came unawares on the enemy concealed in a wood; fortunately for us, he fired too soon, and his eagerness saved us.

Marshal MacMahon, being now of opinion that his corps were too separated, ordered General de Failly to fall back on Beaumont. Unfortunately for us, the enemy had so organized his cordon of *vedettes* that every way was secured, and both officer and despatch fell into his hands. General Douai, however, eventually communicated the order, and the 5th corps marched to Beaumont. This march required great care, as the road that it was necessary to follow lay through a wood and was commanded nearly everywhere.

This was a case, above all others, in which the cavalry should have been sent to the front to examine every wood and hollow, as we had everything to dread. But our confidence was boundless. We started in the dark. The men, worn out with the fatigues of two days of fighting and two night marches, arrived at Beaumont on the 30th, in the middle of a dark night, and, being without a soul to show them where to encamp, they settled down by chance between the forest and the village. In spite of the enemy's vicinity, we bivouacked without our cavalry searching the surrounding country. A wood was close at hand; we neglected to examine it, and it was full of the enemy's artillery and infantry, who, carefully concealed, silently assisted at our installation.

A Prussian officer who was present at this scene afterwards told one of our wounded men that our blind confidence had created a great impression. From their point of observation they could see both officers and men making themselves comfortable, washing, cooking, talking, laughing, and singing, the whole without the least suspicion of who were near them. This officer added that although he was an enemy, he could not help thinking that sometimes in war there were scenes repugnant to a man's better feelings; for instance, he, under cover, would be forced to fire, when he got the order, on a body of men who unsuspectingly laid themselves open to it, and who would shortly be killed like so many sheep.

CHAPTER 4

Battle of Beaumont

About 11 o'clock, in the middle of the tranquillity, whilst some were resting themselves and others were cooking, out burst a storm of fire, and the bivouac was riddled with shot and shell. Everyone started thunderstruck from his tent, rushed to the horses picketed in the lines, and which were loosed with extreme difficulty. The infantry formed up, but in the midst of such confusion it was difficult for the officers to maintain order and cause an effective fire to be opened. The right wing was annihilated and overthrown in the wood. A portion of them rallied on a mound, opposite the village of Mouzon, and, in order to save the remainder of the corps, Béville's brigade was ordered to check the enemy.

This brigade (5th and 6th Cuirassiers) were on the right bank of the Meuse. On receiving the order, they mounted and crossed the river, and, having advanced about) 1,000 yards, they formed up in two lines on the slope of a mound, defended by a *mitrailleuse* battery of the 5th corps; but, immediately this battery opened fire, it was silenced and its pieces dismounted by a storm of shells. At the same time the Prussian infantry decimated our exposed squadrons with their fire. An *aide-de-camp* now galloped up with an order for the 6th Cuirassiers to retire, whilst the 5th were left to hold the enemy in check. The 5th now remained alone, exposed to a perfect hail of shot; some of the bullets, striking with a hard metallic sound, were flattened against the *cuirasses*; others took better effect.

Lieutenant-Colonel Assant was mortally wounded, and the Count de Méautis received a wound in the lower part of his stomach. Wounded men and horses kept falling down in the ranks. The enemy kept advancing nearer and nearer, and his murderous fire swept the Meuse, the bridge, and the fords. It was now, therefore, absolutely necessary, at any sacrifice, to endeavour to check him and stop his fire.

At a command from General Fénélon, the colonel drew sword and led his regiment to the front. Unfortunately, the ground was boggy, uneven, and intersected by a deep ditch. In spite of all this, the *cuirassiers* continued their advance, under fire. The crests of their helmets were either shot away altogether or pierced, epaulettes cut in two, valises torn, and the skirts of tunics with holes in them, so heavy was the fire. The brave Colonel de Contenson was killed, and Commandant Brincourt was also mortally wounded. Besides the field officers, nine troop officers were killed and wounded, and six officers had their horses shot under them; eleven non-commissioned officers and ninety men were placed *hors de combat*. The remains of the 5th Cuirassiers now fell back to the river and tried to cross, with a view to forming up on the opposite bank; but both bridges and fords were blocked up with guns and baggage.

It was therefore determined to swim across the river. Unfortunately, the current was rapid, and it was extremely deep in places. The horses, encumbered by the dreadful weight they had to carry, were scarcely able to swim, and were so done up on reaching the opposite shore that they were unable to climb the banks, and, falling backwards, drowned many of the men with them.

This brilliant example of devoted but useless courage afforded by the 5th Cuirassiers is only another instance of the folly of our old notions that the sole use of cavalry is to charge.

As it could no longer offer an effective resistance, the 5th corps was driven back to Mouzon, where it was under the protection of the 12th, who, thanks to their excellent position, were enabled to hold out until evening.

Marshal MacMahon now saw that he was opposed to such a large force of the enemy that it was useless to think of trying to march to the aid of the Metz army. His right wing had just been driven across the River Meuse, and his left wing no longer rested on the Belgian frontier. To quit the offensive and endeavour to avoid having his retreat cut off was now his sole object, and with this view he issued orders for the army to fall back on Sedan. At the same time he informed the Emperor, who was at Carignan with the 1st corps, of this decision. There was now such a hurry to get ready the emperor's carriages, relays, horses, and baggage that everyone thought a panic had arisen. What sad reflections occur to one when one thinks of the great power once wielded by this sovereign, who, as it were, dictated his wishes to all Europe, and was now sad, and having lost his *prestige*, following his army as it marched to ruin!

The retreat was begun; the night was dark and the roads so blocked up by baggage that the progress of the troops was exceedingly slow. The disorder on every side was now so great that, instead of concealing our march from the enemy, our men lighted torches to show themselves the road, and no one prevented them doing it. Thus the Germans could tell what our object was as well as if we had told them. They followed in our wake, and, as they were perfectly aware of our intentions, they got together all their forces to annihilate us.

CHAPTER 5

Sedan August 31st, September 1st

On the 31st, at about 11 o'clock in the morning, after having passed Douzy, the point of junction of the roads from Mouzon and Carignan to Sedan, General Lebrun's rear guard was attacked by the enemy's cavalry, who threw themselves on the baggage. The terrified drivers cut their traces, overturned the wagons, and our baggage once more fell into the enemy's hands. At the same time there was a sound of heavy firing from the enemy, who were following and attacking our troops. With a view to prevent our retreating beyond Sedan, the Prussians had pushed forward their cavalry and artillery to engage us and thus oblige us to halt. By this manoeuvre they gave the rest of their army time to concentrate for the great battle of the following day.

The same evening a large body of the enemy's cavalry advanced into the plain of Donchéry and thus cut off all communication with Mézières, and as soon as they were certain that we intended to accept the battle, they made the necessary dispositions for surrounding us. One may well ask what our cavalry was doing all this time? Massed in divisions, it marched, each with its own army corps. Not a man was sent out to gain information regarding the enemy's strength and intentions. It was supposed that we had to deal with an army of 60,000; unfortunately, we were opposed to 240,000.

If, in place of leaving the cavalry idle, we had employed it in every direction to maintain our contact with the Prussians, the disaster of Sedan would never have occurred, as the marshal, warned in time, would have retreated to Mézières at all risks. The road to this place was, it is true, guarded by the hostile cavalry, but our own could have attacked them, and would certainly have forced a passage. Instead of playing so brilliant and useful a part, we are about to witness this arm again uselessly devoted to death, and see it vanish in the gulf that already yawned ready to swallow up our whole army.

On the night of the 31st the French divisions were encamped on the right bank of the Meuse and formed a half-circle round Sedan, with the two flanks resting on the river; The troops were drawn up on the hills that command the town on all sides. Sedan, a second-rate fortress, was very badly armed, and, being neither provisioned nor provided with any exterior defences, was incapable of standing a siege, and was therefore incapable of protecting a beaten army. It was for this reason very important for the enemy to arrest us at this point, and, surrounding us during the night with overwhelming forces, he prepared to attack us on both flanks, with a view to uniting, and thus placing us completely at his mercy. Finally, the fire from the artillery that lined the hills on the left bank was in unison with that from the right bank. The King, who was at Vaudresse, now went to Frénois.

At 4 a. m., September 1st, firing was heard in the direction of Bazeilles, which place was occupied by our 12th corps. A heavy fog at this time covered the whole country, and it was impossible to see any distance. General Lebrun, who had given directions the night before to blow up the bridge over the Meuse, could not at first understand how the enemy had crossed. As the firing got heavier, he proceeded to the village, and, as soon as the fog cleared away, saw, to his astonishment, the Bavarians on the right bank of the river.

It will scarcely be credited, but such is the case, that there was no blasting-powder, that the bridge was perfectly intact, and the enemy, profiting by this negligence, had quietly crossed the river. Marshal MacMahon, accompanied by his whole staff and his escort from the 6th Lancers, mounted as soon as he heard the firing; careless of danger, he placed himself in such a prominent position that he at once attracted the enemy's fire. The bullets sowed death on all sides, wounding the officers who stood near, decimating the escort, and the marshal himself was struck by a fragment of a shell. Unwilling to go to the rear, he tried to remain on horseback, but, losing a great deal of blood, he was at last obliged to allow himself to be conveyed to Sedan.

As the marshal's wound was an exceedingly dangerous one, he was unable to keep the command, and accordingly handed it over to General Ducrot. Our new chief, judging correctly that in the position in which we were placed it was impossible to resist the immense masses of the enemy, supported by so formidable an artillery, and seeing that our only hope of safety lay in retreat, issued orders to the officers commanding the various army corps to fall back. General de Wimpfen sent, in answer to this command, an official letter appointing him commander-in-chief. This officer had only arrived from Algeria two days previously, and, not having been present at our reverses, was unaware of our weak points; consequently, taking council only with his own courage, he believed that success was still possible, and considered that at 8 a. m. one should think of victory and not of retreat. General Ducrot's answer to General de Wimpfen was:

I am ready to obey, but allow me, in the name of the country, to beg of you to retreat, and believe me that if we do not do so, it can only lead to disaster.

As, however, it was determined to stand our ground all along the line, we prepared to fight to the last gasp.

We will not enter into all the incidents that took place on this unhappy 1st of September, as the story of the combined operations of the three arms has already been told in the Prussian and French reports. We will only detail the part taken by the cavalry, and also one or two matters that are not generally known, even yet. The general features of the ground, and the position taken up by the French Army, rendered the employment of cavalry extremely difficult. The battle was fought on a half-circle, of which Sedan was the centre. A good deal of manoeuvring on the part of both infantry and artillery was requisite to enable them to take up positions on the arc of the circle, in order to deploy as much as possible. For this reason the cavalry had to be constantly oh the move, to avoid getting in the way of the other arms. On this account also the cavalry attached to an army corps did not invariably remain with it. Thus, the 12th corps had twelve regiments with it at one time.

The most favourable ground was in the direction of Floing, and it is at this point that we shall witness the most serious fighting.

Our army had been fighting since 4 a. m., and were now beginning to tire, and already we could see the circle contracting. On the left General Douai's troops had come in contact at St. Menge with the 4th and 11th Bavarian corps, who had already passed Vrignes-aux-Bois. By degrees fighting began all along the line of hills stretching from Floing to Illy. Our troops had stubbornly resisted this attack from the north, but at last, overwhelmed by the enemy's artillery, they fell back. The cavalry were accordingly now called upon to restore the battle, if possible, by a grand charge.

About 8 a. m. General de Margueritte's division occupied the ground that extends between Floing and the spot occupied by our cavalry at Illy. General de Gallifet's brigade was drawn up in three lines: 1st Chasseurs d'Afrique in the 1st line, the 2nd in support, and the 4th in a third line. General Tillard's brigade (1st Hussars, 6th Chasseurs) was on the right, both regiments in open column.

Bravely led by their officers, our squadrons broke into a gallop, in order to attain the impossible goal to which they were destined; that is to say, the Prussian batteries posted on the heights between St. Menge and Fleigneux. These batteries had in front of them, half way down the hill, two battalions deployed as skirmishers. On seeing us advance, the enemy's infantry, who had not time to form square, nevertheless opened a smart fire, which repulsed the 1st and 3rd Chasseurs d'Afrique. These two regiments now fell back on Illy, and cleared the front for the 4th. This regiment, however, in spite of all its efforts, did not succeed in getting further than the others.

It now changed front, right back, and rejoined the remainder of the division, which was retiring in open column to the wood of Garenne, thus giving way to De Bonnemain's *cuirassiers*, who also suffered some loss. Two squadrons of the 4th Lancers were likewise engaged in this charge. They had bivouacked the previous evening close to Floing, and, on seeing the *Chasseurs d'Afrique* advance, they mounted and moved up in support, and lost about two-thirds of their men and horses.

As the enemy's artillery fire kept increasing in intensity, and had already silenced the battery attached to General de Margueritte's division, the *plateau* now became untenable for our cavalry, who were obliged to fall back in the direction of Sedan. Whilst this retrograde movement was being executed, General Tillard and his galloper were both killed by a bursting shell, just as they got to the wood, behind which the division was formed up in good order, in spite of the losses it had suffered.

About 2 o'clock in the afternoon the fire became so hot and the enemy's infantry advanced in such immense numbers that our infantry was obliged to fall back from the crests of the hills. It was accordingly determined to make another desperate appeal to the devotion of the cavalry, which now, as at every other period of the war, we shall find meeting certain destruction cheerfully. Unfortunately, as usual, it was too late; the only result was a sanguinary and useless sacrifice of men and horses.

General de Margueritte now got together his whole division, consisting of the 1st, 2nd, and 4th Chasseurs d'Afrique, 1st Hussars, and 6th Chasseurs, and advanced upon the heights that lie between Floing and the wood of Garenne. Anxious to examine the ground over which he intended to charge, he advanced bravely to the front, and was mortally wounded on the head by a ball which passed through his cheek and tongue. He handed over the command to General de Gallifet, and passed by us, supported on his horse, by two sergeants-major. His eyes had already begun to dim, his beard was covered with blood, and his hands convulsively grasped the saddle, and, as we gazed on this sad spectacle, each of us regretted this popular leader, who was an ornament to the cavalry, and whose memory will always be dear to us. Placing himself in front of the division, General de Gallifet advanced, with great determination.

Twice these regiments endeavoured to break through the Prussian lines; twice they were obliged to fall back almost annihilated, and with the loss of half their number. The losses were so heavy that the average per regiment of horses killed, wounded, and lost was 240.

The divisions attached to the various army corps also suffered severely from the heavy fire which was poured in on them from all sides. The colonel of the 8th Chasseurs was killed, and General de Fénélon wounded. In this one day our cavalry lost three generals killed and the fourth *hors de combat*.[1]

In spite of the brilliant courage displayed by our cavalry, these charges had no appreciable effect, as the ground was unfavourable ,and the infantry and artillery fire so heavy that half of our squadrons were placed *hors de combat,* without ever being able to reach the enemy. But although the cavalry did not succeed, it has no cause to be ashamed of the part it took on this day, for it preserved the honour of its arms; and, beside the souvenirs of Jena, Friedland, and Eylau, it can inscribe in golden characters the praise bestowed on it by our enemy. In a letter written by the King to the Queen after the Battle of Sedan, His Majesty thus expresses himself:

> I do not know the names of those brave regiments which I saw charge up the heights with a valour beyond all praise. They advanced up the hill, in spite of the fire which more than decimated them, tried to break through our lines, and, falling back, afforded us the sad spectacle of a plain covered with dead and wounded men and horses.

1. Generals de Margueritte, Tirard, and Tillard, killed; General de Fénélon wounded; Colonel Jamin de Fresnay killed.

The American general, Sheridan, who was with the Prussian head-quarters, likewise, in referring to this charge, said that he never, in his experience, had seen any attack so desperate, useless, and sanguinary. The German newspapers also, in writing of this business, give the French cavalry praise, in the following terms:

On a sudden the French cavalry appeared on the scene; it was their last hope, and their attack was intended to take the batteries that were causing them such loss in flank, and also to charge our infantry, who had to withstand the onslaught of *cuirassiers*, hussars, and *Chasseurs d'Afrique*, the latter mounted on splendid barbs. At several points they endeavoured to break our line and thus, open a road for their infantry, but their efforts were repulsed by a cool and well-directed fire, which laid the majority low. Let us give credit to our valiant adversaries, who rushed to death to save, if possible, the rest of their army.

Does not language like the above, when it is used by our enemy, confer praise of the highest description upon our cavalry? After these various attacks, our infantry, being no longer supported, began to give way. The army of the Crown Prince, operating from the west, and that of the Crown Prince of Saxony from the east, now effect a junction at Illy, and from this moment the battle is lost. The Prussian columns now appear on all sides, and drive back our army corps, who no longer offer sufficient resistance to maintain their cohesion. The enemy now crowned the heights, and brought 500 pieces of artillery into action, which concentrated their fire on our worn-out troops.

It was now about half-past three in the afternoon. General de Wimpfen, unwilling for a moment to entertain the idea that the army must surrender, wished to make a last effort. He knew that he had not a chance in his favour, but, provided he could save his honour, this did not signify. He proposed to the Emperor to place himself in the centre of a body of troops which still maintained their order, and with them to break through the enemy. The Emperor answered that he was unable to join him, and sent him a *parlementaire* to propose an armistice.

At the same time a white flag was hoisted on the walls of the town. General de Wimpfen refused to allow the *parlementaire* to pass, and said that he intended to continue the struggle, and proposed to General Lebrun to join him in an attempt to break through the Prussians, or die sword in hand. General Lebrun answered that to attempt such a thing would be madness, but that, if he was determined, he was ready to accompany him. The two generals then drew their swords, and, accompanied by their staff and some soldiers, made the attempt. Their valour was, however, useless, and, seeing the majority of those who accompanied them struck down, they were compelled to relinquish the idea and fall back.

From this moment our troops, beaten at all points, and thrown in disorder by the fire, retreated in confusion. Our men fired off all their remaining cartridges as they fell back, but of what use were they against the concentrated fire of the enemy's artillery? As they could no longer offer any resistance, our troops endeavoured to shelter themselves behind the fortifications and in the ditches, but they could not find a refuge. The shells searched out every spot, killing, wounding, and spreading confusion everywhere.

Whilst the majority of our army was making for Sedan, two squadrons of *cuirassiers* endeavoured to force their way by the Porte de Balan, but it was impossible to do so. On the opposite side Bazeilles was on fire, and the suburb of Balan was occupied by the Bavarians. Unwilling to surrender, the commandant, D'Alincourt, formed column of troops, and, without the least hesitation, advanced at a gallop. Our *cuirassiers* overturned everything that lay in their path; though fired upon from the windows, they kept advancing without losing heart. The enemy, in order to stop them, had barricaded the extremities of the suburb by upsetting some carts. The commandant cleared this obstacle by a desperate leap, but only to fall wounded in the midst of the German guard. The remainder rushed up against the barricade, and, falling one over the other, were shot on the spot; three officers, a veterinary surgeon, and a commissariat officer who had attached himself to them, alone escaped unhurt.

This was the last attempt made by our cavalry, and it reflects credit on it.

At this time the town presented a dreadful appearance. Whilst the battle had been raging outside, Sedan had been overwhelmed by the fire from the artillery posted on the height on the left bank of the Meuse. Knowing their range, these batteries had produced a terrible effect. In one place, the projectiles falling into a courtyard knocked over men and horses waiting the moment to act. Further on, a shell broke into a hospital, knocked to pieces a bed on which lay a wounded officer, and burst in the ward. Terrified and forgetful of their agony, the inmates sought some other place of refuge.

In every direction the same sort of thing was going on. Two generals and several of the inhabitants were killed in the streets. The debris of the various regiments now crowded into the town, and the problem of how to place 80,000 men in a space that would only contain 20,000 arose. The artillery got locked together, the cavalry crowded on to the pavement, and the infantry had to flatten themselves up against the sides of the houses to avoid being crushed to death, and in less than an hour the crowd was so great that it was impossible to either advance or retreat. By seven o'clock in the evening the last shots had been fired, and the drama was finished. The battle had lasted fifteen hours, and our loss was 14,000 killed and wounded.

All around Sedan the villages were on fire, lighting up the field of battle with a sinister glow—this field which was the scene of so much valour, and which was, in spite of it, the resting-place of our glory. From the surrounding heights we could hear the exultant shouts of the enemy. For them the whole was a wild dream of joy; for us a funeral knell. How acutely one feels on occasions like this the meaning of the words Honour and Fatherland, and with what joy one would shed one's blood to ensure victory!

But it was not to be. After having bravely done its duty, the beaten army found itself without the power of continuing the struggle, and that nothing was left to it but capitulation. It is impossible to mention this unhappy event, which struck all France with horror and astonishment, without questioning the judgment of the country, which heaped curses on the prisoners of Sedan, as the circumstances on which the verdict was based are not proved. Eight regiments of cavalry belonging to Marshal MacMahon's army left the field of battle. Their courage has been exalted to the skies, and they have been proudly mentioned as having broken through, at the risk of their lives, the circle of fire that surrounded us. If they acted thus, in accordance with an order they received, they deserve to be handsomely rewarded.

However, it is not our business to discuss at present this matter, the rights of which demand investigation. This business should be enquired into by a commission, as it is important that a question which is so intimately mixed up with military matters should be settled finally. Until the verdict is pronounced, the wisest course is to maintain silence; but if, on the one hand, good taste enjoins silence with respect to those who went away, it also insists that it is our duty to defend those who remained; for, as the former have been praised by this version, the self-respect of the latter have been wounded by it.

The Prussian reports state most distinctly that, once we were surrounded, no body of armed men broke through the circle. Now at 10 a. m. this circle already existed and formed an impassable barrier round the regiments who were on the field of battle. At 2 p. m. a great effort was made by the *chasseurs d'Afrique*, the hussars, the *cuirassiers*, and the lancers. The tributes paid by the King of Prussia, General Sheridan, and the German newspapers are witnesses of the brilliant courage displayed by our cavalry.

In spite of it, however, we failed to pass. At 3:30 p. m. a second effort was made with equal bravery by Generals de Wimpfen and Lebrun, accompanied by a portion of our army. This also was unsuccessful, and they were compelled to fall back, leaving the ground strewn with disabled guns and the dead bodies of men and horses. Finally, somewhat later on, a last effort was made by the *cuirassiers*. We have seen how they were stopped by the barricade and killed almost to a man, without being able to break through. All these attempts were unsuccessful, it is true, but what more could these brave regiments, who encountered death so fearlessly, effect?

They did not break through, certainly, but they have reason to be proud of not having left the field of battle, of having remained where their duty required them, obedient to the orders of the commander-in-chief; charging home when called upon to do so, taking part up to the last in a desperate game, and devoting themselves cheerfully without a thought for the consequences.

Such was the *rôle* of the prisoners of Sedan; their only wish is to be fairly judged, for the better it is known what their behaviour was on this occasion, the more will their devotion to a flag so obstinately betrayed by fortune be appreciated. We have but few words to add to complete the history of the cavalry on this campaign. It is with a gloomy sadness that one continues this recital, for the last drops in the cup are the most bitter.

The commands of our conqueror are received. All we have is to be given up, and, in order not to lose any of his trophies, he promises more favourable terms if they are given up intact. On the receipt of this intelligence we were all filled with rage, and the men were animated with the same feelings. The troops refuse to give up their arms, and, despising reprisals, they set to work to break up everything.

Pistols, swords, *cuirasses*, lances, are all dashed to pieces; the saddles are destroyed, and the fragments thrown about; the guidons are burnt. Soon the streets were filled with the debris, and the town resembled a sea-shore where there had been a shipwreck. We were given, as a rendezvous, the village of Iges, which lies at the extremity of the angle formed by the Meuse. Sadly and silently the regiments wend their way to this strip of cursed land.

Try to imagine all that there is most repugnant in misery, everything that is pestilent and wretched, and you will form but a faint conception of the privations we had to endure. Night came on, we march on our way without knowing where to halt, and keep swaying backwards and forwards; our unhappy soldiers are without either food, shelter, or clothing. We were obliged to remain in the open, and the rain fell in torrents. Deep in mud, without cloaks and with our clothes worn out, we crowd together for warmth. Hunger now assailed us with its pangs. We likewise began to suffer from thirst, for, though the Meuse was at hand, its waters were corrupted by the numberless corpses that floated in it.

The horses had to undergo the same sort of sufferings, and, in consequence, the disorder was dreadful. One has often heard, of the immense herds of wild horses that gallop about the plains of America. For miles they say the earth trembles with the tread of their hoofs, and these wild bands, like a hurricane that has broken loose, overthrow all in their path.

At Iges the same sort of thing occurred. There were still 10,000 horses belonging to the cavalry. In order to avoid giving them up to the enemy, their picketing-ropes had been cut, and the horses, galloping in every direction, soon left no place where one was out of their reach; deprived of their usual food, they commenced to fight, and tore each other to pieces, and then for a change rushed down to the river at such a pace that the foremost were driven into the water and drowned, and the river encumbered with their bodies. For four days we did not die outright of hunger, but merely existed in this hideous swamp, into which we had been cast, and which more nearly resembled Dante's Inferno than any other spot.

How can we ever forget these scenes? Our cavalry, which scarcely a month ago was so brilliant, so confident in itself and careless of danger, so devoted when called upon to sacrifice itself, was now completely broken down. We have already related how the cavalry of the Metz army melted away by degrees, until at the end of October it disappeared altogether; defeat did not spare them any more than ourselves, and their last state was as pitiable as our own. But the remembrance of their valour will live forever, for their deeds are inscribed in the blood they everywhere poured out so freely.

Such was the part taken by the French cavalry of the Army of the Rhine. The lesson we have received is a bitter one; the more reason is there, therefore, that we should profit by it, and, with this object in view, we propose to deduct, in the following pages, from past events, what should be the drill and instruction our cavalry should receive.

PART 4

CHAPTER 1

The Rôle of the Cavalry Before an Action

The German authorities on this subject assert that the part taken by the cavalry on the day of battle is not their most important function. Often, indeed, it is but a subordinate one. If the opportunity of charging occurs, naturally, it must not be neglected; but its delicate and indispensable role is on the eve of battle, when it must reconnoitre, establish contact with the enemy, keep up communications between the various army corps, and spread itself like a curtain, behind which the commander-in-chief manoeuvres his troops and makes the necessary disposition for a general action.

With such tactics, intelligently put in practice, Germany commenced hostilities. Her scouts, far in advance, pushed on until they came in contact with the enemy. As soon as this contact (Fühling) was once established, it was never lost. Thus the enemy could not make the slightest movement without the cognizance of the commander-in-chief. To properly carry out such a system as the above, one must have intelligent troops, and it is only fair to state that the instruction imparted by Prussia to her cavalry in peace-time had prepared them in the best possible manner for the service she demanded of them in war. We shall find proofs of this assertion at every period of the campaign. From the very first, the Prussian cavalry advanced onto our territory in small bodies, to study our positions. Better acquainted with the country than we were, they were enabled to advance without hesitation.

Both at Wissembourg and Woerth the enemy's scouts discovered and reported that our numbers were small, and that we should be annihilated by being outnumbered. Throughout our retreat they followed us step by step, watching us ceaselessly, giving an exact detail of our halts, times of departure, marches, obliging us by the daring way in which they pushed ahead to alter our route, appearing only to disappear, and remaining the whole time perfectly unassailable. For a very short time, certainly, in the plains of Champagne, the Prussian staff missed us, because we suddenly changed our plans; but by means of their cavalry, who never again lost the contact, and who marched on our flank, deployed like a curtain behind which their army could work, they soon recovered the lost thread.

When we were at Chêne Populeux, the enemy was covered for ten leagues in advance by his cavalry. As we advanced we kept meeting little groups of five or six men together, who retired slowly and only after ascertaining our movements, etc., which information they immediately communicated to those in rear. If we had followed them up, each group would have fallen back until they reached a support strong enough to resist, and then opposed us, in order to prevent our breaking through the curtain and getting at their main body. This service was so intelligently performed by the Prussian cavalry that we marched as it were in a net, in the meshes of which we were eventually entangled.

There is a striking difference between the above and our way of acting. With the Metz army, just as much as with the Strasbourg army, we shall see the same distinctive feature—heroic valour, but, in that lay the whole of our science. The outposts were so badly posted that the cavalry were placed behind the infantry; and this was our best means of keeping guard. In place of keeping up a perpetual contact by means of one or two men or by small detachments advancing continuously and keeping as much under cover as possible, we carried out our reconnaissances with one or two squadrons, or even with a regiment that proceeded in such a way that all could see what was going on. These reconnaissances, no doubt, were ordered to proceed to long distances, but often they returned and reported that they could see nothing of the enemy.

What then happened? Why, that our enemy was following us only a mile or two off, and as soon as we were asleep, or not on the lookout, overwhelmed us with shot and shell in our bivouacs.

In this manner we were surprised, both at Wissembourg and Beaumont.

At Vionville the horses were being watered when the enemy's artillery opened fire. At Woerth our commander-in-chief had such bad information that he imagined he was opposed to 40,000, in place of which he had to contend against 140,000. The same thing occurred at Sedan. During the night the enemy's forces were trebled, and we were surrounded by 240,000 men, without anybody having the least notion of what was going on. These examples are sufficient to demonstrate that we have much to learn in the art of reconnoitring. We have been repeatedly told that the regulations for outpost duty contain all the necessary rules for service, but that we have not studied them sufficiently.

According to us, this is not quite correct; our regulations on outposts are very far from laying down what is the best method to obtain useful information regarding an enemy. The regulations lay down a line of *vedettes*, outlying and inlying pickets, reconnoiterers, and patrols, who keep going out and returning from time to time; all this is very well for an army that is simply on the defensive. But this system is altogether insufficient for an army with an offensive *rôle*, for if you are satisfied to obtain information regarding an enemy by pushing forward reconnaissances, to any distance you like, but which merely come back and report what they have seen, the situation may change during every second they are occupied in returning, and the reports, perfectly exact at the time they were made, will often be nothing when received but a mass of fatal errors. In order to avoid reporting what is not the case, it is absolutely indispensable to establish a contact, and we will now endeavour to lay down how this should be done.

In what part of our regulations can you find it laid down how to form an impenetrable curtain behind which the army may manoeuvre quietly and unseen? Nevertheless, this is one of our most important duties. In proof of this, the following instance, selected from the Prussian reports, will suffice:

> On the Loire, Prince Frederick Charles, finding his troops done up, deployed his cavalry, and, concealed behind this curtain, and by making feints at Bourbaki and Chanzy, he was enabled to give his army eight days' rest, during which they were served out with uniforms, boots, and provisions; and as soon as they had been completely rested and reinforced, he withdrew his cavalry, placed it on the flanks, and confided to his artillery the duty of annihilating us.

A similar example is furnished by the Metz army. After the battle of Rézonville, whilst the French army was still in the neighbourhood of the battlefield, the enemy's cavalry maintained their contact continuously, covering with troops the ground that was to be the scene of action on the following day, and forming themselves into an impenetrable curtain, masking the movements of both the German armies, and thus permitting them to unite without the fear of being disturbed, and allowing them to execute, on the morning of the 17th, a change of front to the right, with Gravelotte for a pivot.

The same sort of tactics were pursued throughout the march of the Crown Prince and the Crown Prince of Saxony to Sedan. In every direction we had bad information concerning the enemy's movements, because he carefully concealed himself behind the curtain formed by his cavalry. These novel ideas had brought into practice, in the Prussian Army, a system of tactics which was entirely unknown in our regulations. As, besides all this, the enemy, possessed a most perfect knowledge of the country, our cavalry found itself in a position so much inferior that no valour, however brilliant, was sufficient to counterbalance its deficiencies in these important particulars. It is not a difficult matter to make ourselves as good as the enemy, but to do so, it must be allowed we have much to learn.

CHAPTER 2

Role During the Action

It is generally admitted that the employment of cavalry against unbroken infantry or artillery in position, owing to the increased range of firearms, is impossible. The study of this war, however, furnishes us with numerous examples of engagements undertaken under such conditions. It is, however, sufficient to examine these cases to prove to oneself that the annihilation of troops engaged in such an enterprise is almost certain, and that without producing any result.

At Froeschwiller cavalry were sent, at different stages of the battle, against victorious infantry and artillery. On this occasion the various regiments advanced in succession, charged over unoccupied ground, and retired after suffering fabulous losses, without ever using their sabres and without ever getting at the enemy. The natural result was a repulse, without even a chance of success.

At Beaumont, the same conditions and the same result. At Sedan the cavalry charged with the courage of despair, against infantry and artillery. The enemy waited for them without moving, and annihilated our regiments, who retired after losing half their numbers and without having succeeded in checking their fire. At Rézonville the *cuirassiers* of the Guard charged Prussian squares. They were broken to pieces against the squares, left the greater part of their number on the ground, and failed to break the enemy. Thus, in every instance, undeniable valour, accompanied by enormous losses and want of appreciable result.

Now, for the other side of the argument; we have often heard quoted the charge made by von Bredow's brigade of the Duke William of Mecklenburg's division.[1] If you refer to the details of this

1. Evidently an error. Von Bredow's brigade belonged to von Rheinbaben's division.—A. L. W.

charge, such as we have given them, you will see that the conclusion is similar. This charge against our infantry and artillery was made by two lines of *cuirassiers* and lancers in *échelon*. Before the advance, the enemy took the indispensable precaution, that we invariably neglected, of silencing our artillery with his. Nevertheless, if we examine the results obtained, we shall see that, though their squadrons undoubtedly broke through our lines, sabering all in their path, on their falling back, they were literally cut to pieces by our dragoons and *cuirrassiers*; and, setting aside the glory of the charge, the success was more imaginary than real, since our infantry was not routed and our artillery did not lose a single gun.

From the examples that have been quoted it would seem natural to conclude that the role of the cavalry on a battlefield has been diminished; but this is far from being the case, and it will be shown that its part, more intimately connected with artillery, owing to the increased range of that arm, is, although different, more important than ever. We have seen it fail, notwithstanding the most brilliant valour, because it was only employed against the front and after all else had failed. Would the result have been the same had it been employed in extending a position, in flanking movements on a grand scale, and in advancing far to the front, combined with artillery, of which arm it would have been the only possible support? This question it is proposed to answer by an examination of our various engagements.

At Froeschwiller the battle at 2 p.m. was still undecided, and this was the moment at which the enemy tried to out flank us; 35,000 men were about to try conclusions with 140,000, and our right wing was our weak point. We might have remedied this and made up for our numerical inferiority by extending a long line of cavalry. There were ten regiments of cavalry belonging to the 1st corps; two only were on the left wing, and the remainder were aimlessly distributed about the centre and amongst the infantry divisions. They charged positions in front and were unsuccessful.

It is permissible to suppose that the result might have been different had we responded to the enemy's flanking movement by a similar one. At the time when their columns advanced, winding along the hills, in order to outflank us, if we had sent out artillery, supported by the whole of our cavalry, on to their flank, we might have checked their advance and secured to our army time to fall back. The officer commanding; the 4th division entertained this idea; for he issued orders to that effect, but he wanted sufficient materials, and he was obliged to content himself with disputing foot by foot the ground he occupied. It was impossible on this occasion to anticipate success, but still our army would have been able to beat an orderly retreat, whilst as it was it was routed.

At Beaumont, likewise, our cavalry was thrown away, because it was obliged to attack straight to its front, and came across bad ground, whilst, if it had been allowed to turn the hill, it would have acted on an easier piece of ground. Circumstances at Sedan were quite exceptional. It was impossible to deploy and extend the flanks, because we had to fight on a circle, the two ends of which rested on a river. For this reason the regiments kept constantly on the move, like the needle of a compass, turning in every direction, and never still. In studying the evens of this day, so fatal to the French arms, we shall discover an incident which will prove better than all commentary the immense benefit to be derived from a combination of cavalry and artillery.

The colonel of Prussian hussars who came to take over Sedan stated that for several hours the 200 guns which caused us such damage were supported by his regiment alone. His anxiety for a long time was intense, as, had anything happened, he could have afforded but little help. Accordingly, in order to convey the impression that he had a large body of troops at his disposal, he showed himself along the crests of the various heights, and thus displayed a continuous line, which seemed to extend for some distance. What a splendid success might have been achieved had our cavalry been launched against the regiment that supported those guns!

The battle of Rézonville demonstrates the utility of cavalry when it is employed on the flank. Threatened by a grand flank attack on the part of the enemy, General de Ladmirault hastily assembled the cavalry that was near, and, thrusting it boldly forward, succeeded in extricating the right of the army, and remained master of the field. This was, on the whole, successful; but the general has often stated that this indecisive success might have been changed into a complete victory had he had a large cavalry force, fresh and ready, formed up to be employed at the right moment. In place of this, the cavalry was divided into four distinct divisions, each under a separate officer.

In one place, Generals du Barail and Legrand; further off, General de France, with the lancers and dragoons of the Guard, who were merely there by accident, as they were returning from escorting the Emperor, as hard as they could go; lastly, close to Bruville, was General de Clérembault. As this large body of cavalry was not launched in the desired direction with a common object, as each commanding officer was his own master, and as each had his own individual ideas, naturally the orders issued by the commandant of the 4th corps lost in power and rapidity of execution.

Indeed, it was necessary to explain to each officer separately the wishes of General de Ladmirault; then the charges were executed one after another, owing to the want of a directing hand, and when the recall was sounded for the guards, it was mistaken by the other regiments for a general recall, and they also accordingly fell back.

As for de Clérembault, who was near Bruville, not having been informed of what was about to occur, he only guessed at the great action that was taking place from seeing the heavy clouds of dust raised by the combatants. He immediately advanced, but only came up at the end of the fighting. His division consisted of five regiments; such a force charging at the proper moment would certainly have altered the result.

General de Ladmirault has, therefore, a perfect right to assert that he would have obtained a complete victory in place of a partial success had he had from the commencement of the action this large body of cavalry at his disposal, drawn up in the rear of the right wing, and ready to charge at the right moment under the immediate orders of a single general who completely understood the object to be attained.

From the Battle of Rézonville we learn the importance of turning movements, and the power of cavalry acting on the flanks. We shall find further confirmation of this in the following actions.

The part taken by our cavalry in this battle (Gravelotte) was unimportant, because the various divisions (*viz.*, Guards, de Forton's, de Valabrègue's in other words, the majority of our cavalry) were massed in the grounds of Lessy,[2] Chatel St. Germain, and Moulin Longeau, where they were under fire without having the power to act. We will therefore enquire whether or no they might have been usefully employed on our extreme right on the open ground in front of St. Privat and Roncourt. The ground on the right of our position was the only portion of the battlefield where cavalry could act. At this point then, naturally, our cavalry should have been concentrated the previous evening, on the banks of the River Orne, in the villages of St. Marie-aux-Chênes, St. Ail, Batilly, and Habonville. They would have had excellent accommodation, a large open plain, and ground firm enough to work over in every direction.

---

2. East of Gravelotte.

Placed in this position, the cavalry would have been able to give information regarding the great turning movement carried out by the enemy on the 18th, with the assistance of his cavalry. Let us now turn to what the enemy's cavalry did. It did not execute a number of charges against our position, but, accompanied by artillery, it preceded the movement of their left wing in its great march, the object of which was a change of front to the right. It thus covered the deployment of the columns of infantry, in the grounds of Batilly and St. Ail, before their attack on St. Privat.

If our cavalry, together with the horse artillery, had acted in a similar manner, they would have been able to delay the march of the enemy sufficiently to prevent their attaining their object before the end of the battle, and would have succeeded in engaging the enemy's cavalry, who, as it was, were able to do what they liked. If the divisions of Desvaux, de Forton, and de Valabrègue, useless in the positions which they occupied, had been employed in the manner already indicated (*viz.*, in front of our right wing), they would have enabled us to take the offensive with this wing, and this movement would have been supported by the two divisions of cavalry posted in rear of the 3rd and 4th corps, and who had no opportunity of acting, as we remained on the defensive.

On the 31st August and 1st September our cavalry was not employed, but it might have rendered assistance to our right wing had it been employed on the Sarrelouis and St. Avoid roads. Preceded by the artillery, of which it would have been the support, it might have accompanied the advance of Bastoul's division of the 2nd corps, and been supported on their right by Castagny's division of the 3rd corps. In this case, as at Rézonville and Gravelotte, it was an offensive and flanking movement of our right wing that would have ensured success; to this place, therefore, we should have taken our cavalry, more especially as the ground was favourable.

From the preceding examples it is natural to conclude that the importance of cavalry is not diminished, but only that it is not expedient to employ this arm in the manner we did during this campaign.

We must look for the best results to movements in extension of the line and to flank movements.

In all these battles it was on the flanks that our cavalry might have taken a brilliant and decisive share had it been concentrated, in place of being split up into useless fractions.

As regards charges, with the exception of those undertaken against cavalry, experience shows that regiments that attack straight to the front almost invariably suffer enormously, without gaining any reasonable success. Let us avoid, therefore, wasting our courage in this useless manner.

This leads us to consider a matter of some importance.

When a cavalry division is called upon to charge, the regulations lay it down as a rule that the general in command should place himself in front to lead. What is the result of such a rule? Why, that whilst the general is engaged in the *mêlée* there is nobody to follow the varying chances of the engagement, and sound the recall if we are getting the worst of it, or, on the other hand, organize a pursuit. In proof of this you may cite the general charge at Rézonville.

General Legrand bravely led his division into action; wounded in several places, he fell to rise no more. His division continued its course, joined in the *mêlée*, and there was no one to either direct the fight or order a recall.

The consequence was, a mistake occurred—a recall was sounded for a portion of the combatants, and was understood to be for the whole.

Then there is the reserve that every body of cavalry should have. Who is to lead it? Who is to judge of the proper moment for charging, and in what direction it should advance? Nevertheless, it is the reserve that ensures success.

The charge at Rézonville is a proof of this also. Our regiments were giving way when the colonel of the 4th Dragoons came up just at the end of the engagement, attacked the enemy with a single squadron, and forced the latter first to fall back to the heights, and finally to retreat altogether.

Therefore, according to us, the place of an officer who commands a body of cavalry sufficiently strong to have a reserve is not at the head of that body in the charge. He ought to hand over his duty to the second in command. As for himself, his business is to watch the battle, ready to employ his reserve either in support of the weak point, to ensure victory, or cover a retreat.

It will be difficult to break through this old custom, as it has a chivalrous side which corresponds with the national character. But if the position is less brilliant in appearance, it has the advantage of being more practical, and should therefore be adopted.

CHAPTER 3

Role After a Battle

If an army is victorious, the employment of cavalry does not require discussion, as its part evidently is to pursue vigorously and harass the enemy in every possible way; but if an army is retreating, the place of cavalry can no longer be in the rear as formerly. Cavalry, being unable to contend alone against long-range artillery, would soon find itself crushed and dispersed if it was taken in rear or on the flank by a numerous artillery, and this might produce irremediable confusion amongst the troops in front.

The Metz army affords us a conclusive argument in favour of what we advance.

On the 7th the whole of the cavalry division of General de Clérembault was ordered to cover the retreat of the 3rd corps, which was to leave St. Avold for Metz on the 8th. From St. Avold to Longeville, a distance of some three miles, the road passes between woods, which in some places almost touch the road, and in others leave open ground sufficient to deploy a small body of troops. At Longeville the road separates, and to the left passes over a moderately broad *plateau*.

The division was composed of four regiments of dragoons (2nd, 4th, 5th, and 8th). The two regiments belonging to Juniac's brigade were sent to Forbach, and returned on the morning of the 8th; in addition to these regiments, there were three regiments of *chasseurs* (2nd, 3rd, and 10th). The 3rd were detached with the 1st infantry division of the 3rd corps. General de Clérembault had therefore six regiments. The general perceived that the least mishap to a rear guard thus constituted might lead to the most fatal result, as he was unable to act on the sides of the road; he therefore informed Marshal Bazaine several times of this fact; *viz.*: that such a large body of cavalry, under the circumstances, was more harm than good.

The marshal did not consider it necessary to attend to these observations, and, according to the original arrangement, the retreat commenced at 3:30 a. m., on the 8th. Three divisions of infantry (Grenier's of 4th corps, Castagny's and Decaen's of the 3rd) were in close column on the road. In rear of these was a long train of hired transports, which stretched to an interminable extent, owing to its slow and irregular march.

During the whole time this column was filing by, the cavalry, to the great fatigue of both men and horses, had to remain in the low ground about St. Avold, and this without being of the slightest use, as it was impossible for them to prevent a flank attack.

It was 1 p. m. before the cavalry was able to move off. They were now disposed in *échelon*, on both sides of the road. Looking towards the frontier, there was only space sufficient to deploy a single squadron. A battery of horse artillery, placed under the orders of the general, was in position at a point commanding the valley of St. Avold. By 2 p.m. Decaen's division had completely evacuated its position. From this moment the cavalry was alone in rear to protect the retreat, and, owing to the ground, it was soon obliged to take to the road, and, quitting its offensive formation, break into a column of route which stretched its length through twenty-four squadrons. In front the infantry and baggage train proceeded slowly and with a certain amount of disorder.

It is easy to imagine what would have been the result of all this had a single Prussian battery of artillery taken up a position on the heights that command St. Avold, and had opened fire on this long line of cavalry, which had no means of defending itself, and which would have been deprived of the support of even its own battery of artillery, as the position occupied by the battery would have been commanded by the enemy's guns. In, spite of all the courage and presence of mind that it is possible to imagine, by reason of being attacked without the possibility of retaliation, confusion would have ensued, the march would have insensibly augmented from the rear of the column to the front, and once disorder in the ranks had occurred, the drivers of the wagons would have taken fright, and would have brought about a regular panic.

This danger was not realized, as the Prussians did not make their appearance until we reached the *plateau* of Longeville; but we may gather from this a lesson, and conclude that that ground is exceptional which permits cavalry to cover a retreat. The duty of covering a retreat belongs rather to the infantry, covered by skirmishers, who will retire slowly, taking advantage of the ground, and be supported by artillery in commanding positions. All through the campaign we find cases to support this theory. Whenever cavalry charged, the enemy's infantry hardly ever took the trouble to form square. A deployed formation was sufficient to repel an attack, which formation was then supported by the skirmishers on the flanks, who advanced to take the cavalry in rear and on the flank.

Under these circumstances the *rôle* of the cavalry in a retreat is *nil*, and it is preferable to employ it on the flanks to oppose that of the enemy and prevent them seizing convoys and cutting in between the columns.

PART 5

Future Employment of Cavalry

After the incidents we have narrated, it is easy to indicate the future use of cavalry, and the instruction it should receive. The basis of instruction is as before, but the manner of application is different.

If it is necessary to give intelligence, it is indispensable to establish a contact and be acquainted with the least of the enemy's movements, and, as we have already shown, to attain this, our passive system of outposts is not sufficient; a more active and intelligent system is indispensable to meet this necessity. The needful system is to get into contact, far in advance of the army one covers, and, according to the German notions, the following is the way to do so:

A few men, at long distances from each other, advance until they meet the enemy. As soon as the contact is established, it must be maintained until a general engagement is brought on. At about a mile and a half from these small parties, small pickets are disposed in support of them. These are detached from one or two squadrons, who are still further in rear, say at a distance of one or one and a half miles. And lastly, the regiments to which these; detachments belong come some distance in rear.

This is the general outline of the system. As for its working, it is necessary to trust to those in front.

It is not only necessary to guard against surprise, but also to fathom the enemy's intentions, to understand his dispositions, numbers, and future plans. The fate of great operations depends on the accuracy of these reports, and the important duty of furnishing them should not be entrusted to privates. A staff officer, whose special duty should be to reconnoitre the enemy, accompanied by some officers and men chosen from the cavalry, the whole mounted on good horses, in order that they may pass rapidly along the line and collect reports and information, should, after verifying the reports, forward them to the officer commanding.

Protected in this manner, all surprise will be impossible; every movement of the enemy will be immediately known, and the work of the commander-in-chief simplified, as he will be able to form his plans, modify them, and dispose his troops in perfect security, and in taking as much time as he needs.

For troops who are stationary and on the lookout it is indispensable that a regular system of patrols, who should proceed beyond the extreme advanced points, should be organized in such a manner as to keep up a continual movement of parties coming in and going out, so that no change may take place in the extreme front without the body from which these parties are sent out being immediately informed of it.

To carry out this duty efficiently you must employ at least a third of your party. It is also necessary to lay down an exact detail of duties, as on this condition only will your horses obtain the rest necessary to enable them to undertake long marches.

It is not necessary for us to enter into these details, as they would only make one lose sight of the general idea that it is desired to sketch. The same observation applies to the method of disposing the cavalry as a screen, as well as to the proper manner of occupying, with parties continually increasing in strength; villages, open towns, branch lines of railway, etc.

If we now turn to the employment of cavalry during an action, the incidents of this war will prove that charges to the front[1] produce but small results, and that whilst waiting for an opportunity to charge, which may perhaps never occur, it is unwise to place your cavalry in such a position that they cannot be of the slightest use. From this it also seems necessary to conclude that the small bodies of cavalry who are attached to army corps should only be attached with the understanding that they may be withdrawn should the ground prove unfavourable to their action, as, indeed, was done on the 31st and 1st.

Judging from all these examples, it seems incontestable that during a battle the real place of cavalry is the flanks, and Woerth, Rézonville, and Gravelotte prove this.

A large field for the employment of cavalry is also opened up by the introduction of rifled artillery. A splendid part may be played by the artillery undertaking flank movements on a large scale, out of

---

1. It is important to remember that in all MacMahon's battles the German cavalry never attempted such charges, but were invariably kept out of range.

sight, and appearing suddenly in the rear or flanks of an enemy, and thus throw them into confusion. But in marches such as these artillery is neither able to reconnoitre nor to defend itself, unless, indeed, they leave their guns to themselves. It is therefore indispensable that they should have a support against a surprise or attack on the part of the enemy. This support must be furnished by the cavalry exclusively, on account of its mobility.

Whilst the guns are in action the cavalry should keep as much as possible out of the line of fire, at the same time being near enough to defend the artillery in case of necessity. But from the distances from which artillery now comes into action the enemy's cavalry can alone pretend to attack it. Under these circumstances the two bodies of cavalry will meet in the charge, and one will often see, notwithstanding all that history says on this subject, that neither will avoid the shock, but act as they did at Rézonville. In a case of this description it must be borne in mind that, supposing the chances on both sides are equal, the heavy cavalry will get the best of it.

We must therefore conclude that the more important artillery becomes, the greater will the part of the cavalry be also, as these two arms are necessary to each other, and from a combination of them will arise a number of movements which will enable one to undertake the most daring enterprises.

What can afford a more striking instance of this than the case of 200 guns, supported only by one regiment of hussars, that played upon us with such terrible effect at Sedan? Our fortunate enemy has demonstrated to us all the advantage to be obtained from cavalry properly commanded. Let us imitate his example. Before the war, much was written and said in France in support of the theory that the importance of cavalry had diminished, and that this arm ought to be reduced.

Better informed and more clear-sighted Prussia allowed us to theorize, silently prepared her own cavalry, increased its numbers and its relative proportion to the other arms, and appeared on the field of battle with new tactics, and thus reaped the reward it deserved. Listen to what the German papers say with respect to this arm:

> Have not they who asserted that a return of the glorious days of Ziethen and Seidlitz was impossible fallen into a terrible mistake? And what gratitude we owe to our royal general, who, unmoved by any opposition fearful of expense, foresaw that, in spite of *mitrailleuse* and rifled firearms, it was necessary to

increase the cavalry. Thus he collected such a force of this arm that the world has never seen its equal. Everybody now understands that without our scouts the bold and rapid advance of the Crown Prince would have been impossible. What person in Prussia could now be found to deny the importance of cavalry? Who, in face of the results obtained, could be found to oppose with idiotic stupidity our army budget, drawn up by competent military men? Let him cast an eye on Alsace and Lorraine and the work there performed by the cavalry.

At the same time that the Prussian press wrote with such conviction—a conviction brought about by actual events, a French pamphlet demanded the reduction of the cavalry by half. There you have the whole lesson that we have learnt from this war. Nevertheless, the lesson was sufficiently bitter to prevent one's desiring a repetition of it.

The indisputable fact—and it is a fact that cannot be too much impressed upon our cavalry—is that they have much to learn and many reforms to undergo. The regulations of 1829 still held good under the Empire. Perfect at the time they were originally drawn up, they no longer meet modern requirements. Let us ask, is it possible, is it probable, that whilst infantry, and artillery, and every branch of the service, in short, has, during these forty years, undergone various complete transformations, the cavalry alone should have remained, like the heavenly bodies, perfect and incapable of improvement? Thus, from the commencement of hostilities, the weakness of every part of our organization became only too apparent.

Owing to our system of remounts, we were obliged, for want of reserves, to march with a strength that was barely sufficient for a peace establishment; and, once on the road, our squadrons of 80 horses remained at that strength without ever being completed up to their proper total. Therefore, we must reorganize and perfect this branch of our system. An improved system should supply an inexhaustible supply of Amounts told off to regiments beforehand, and which should be numerous enough to fill up all vacancies. The same thing applies to the teaching of both man and horse.

If you turn to the way the soldier has been taught, you see that from the first our army learns from its reverses that it has had bad information, and that no contact has been established with the enemy. Continually drilled in masses, we are incapable of acting in an isolated fashion. But the principal things which showed our deficient instruction were our ignorance of the country, inability to read a map rapidly, and to find the most direct roads and choose the shortest bridle-paths. In former days it was supposed that physical force was more necessary to a cavalry soldier than intelligence.

This is no longer the case. This; campaign has proved that courage is not everything—that an intelligent system of instruction in reading maps, etc., is absolutely indispensable; in addition to this, rapidity, dash, and ruse in discovering an enemy; watch him ceaselessly, discover his plans, and defeat his projects by one's own combinations. Let us therefore combine together to undertake for the future the part that it is necessary we should take. We shall attain this result by ceasing to make numberless and intricate movements the groundwork of our drill. From the month of February up to the annual inspection—that is to say, during the most seasonable months—we spend our whole time in drilling in masses; everything else is merely accessory.

Without doubt it is of the utmost importance that a regiment should be able to manoeuvre rapidly, and maintain order whilst doing so; but one-third of the movements prescribed in our cavalry regulations are ample to attain this end. This abuse of the drill-ground, and this mathematical exactitude, brought to bear on alignments, etc., all marked out beforehand, restrict our freedom of action and habituate us to work in a confined manner, whilst really the cavalry soldier is destined to work over a large tract of country, and ride to any spot he can see in the distance, and to enable him to do so he has his horse, which is his principal arm.

As to the powers of a troop horse, it is not too much to assert that, as they have been but little studied, but little is known of them. If we are to judge by the regulations that rule us,—and as long as they are in force to them must we turn for what we are to believe,—we shall form a curious idea of these powers.

The pace of a horse was originally fixed by the range of the firearm in use at that time. This weapon had a range of some 200-250 yards, and the pace was calculated for this distance. It was even imagined that there was danger in attempting to gallop this distance, and, in order to avoid blowing a horse, it was laid down that about 85 yards should be the distance over which one might charge, and the remainder of the ground was to be traversed at a walk, a trot, and a gallop.

Everyone knows that the regulation rapidity of these paces is as follows:

Walk	100 yards per minute.
Trot	240 yards per minute.

Gallop 300 yards per minute.

Charge 150 in 20 seconds, or 450 per minute.

As there was no question of staying power,—that is to say, the greatest distance for which these paces could be maintained,—the figures given above constitute all that is laid down, and these figures have not been altered for the last forty years, (at time of first publication).

It must be allowed that statistics like the above are not calculated to convey an exaggerated opinion of the power of cavalry to an officer ignorant of that arm, and who wished to study it.

There is a prevalent suspicion, however, it is true, that a horse's powers exceed these narrow limits; but this, of course, is merely supposition.

Some people, referring to the fabulous distances traversed by African horses, lay down marches of 120 leagues in forty hours as quite natural. Others, putting their faith in thoroughbreds, consider steeplechases of four miles over a fair hunting country as mere child's play. Others, again, talk lightly of eighteen to twenty miles at an unbroken trot or gallop.

Between such marvels of endurance and speed and what the regulations tell us, how are we to arrive at the truth? Without horses there can be no cavalry. The horse is the real weapon of the cavalry soldier, and we are ignorant of the powers of this weapon. This being the case, how can anyone pretend to regulate its proper employment? If you went and said to the infantry or artillery, "Here is a capital rifle or gun, the powers of which are something tremendous, but we are ignorant both of the range and trajectory, but that does not matter, you can use it," they would most assuredly reply, "No, thank you: we don't care about arms that will leave us uncertain in face of an enemy." Such, however, is the situation of the cavalry, and we wish to know if you can find an answer to the following questions in any book whatever:[2]

What is the average of the extreme powers of staying of a troop horse?

How often can he charge successively?

In what condition is he after marching 9, 12, 18, 24, 36 miles at a fair pace?

How should the pace be regulated so as to allow a given dis-

---

2. This portion of the work was written before the war, but it was not allowed to be published.

tance to be traversed and bring your horse up fresh to charge? What influence has the weight on his back on his staying powers and speed?

What are the results of a gradual increase in the ration?

The day these questions are answered and laid down in the regulations, our cavalry will have made a great step in advance, for just as great discoveries have introduced great destructive engines of mathematical precision, so also have they fixed their powers. Then the generals under whose orders we may be placed will know exactly what they can expect, and we shall cease to be sometimes a bore and at others a deception.

From the foregoing considerations we may conclude that it is indispensable for the cavalry to introduce reforms into all the matters that concern it, such, for instance, as recruiting, remounts, and the drill and instruction of both man and horse.

So as not to overstep the limits of this work, the object of which was to give a true account of the part taken by the cavalry in this campaign, we shall at some other time treat separately each of the above, subjects.

Conclusion

The history of this campaign is a very sad one for France. Would that it were possible to strike out of our annals this funeral page and bury forever those mournful recollections, whose accents seem to murmur in our ears like a death chant. But though we are wounded to the quick by the defeats that have fallen on us, nevertheless we have the right to be proud of our energy in misfortune. Our neighbours looked on with folded arms at the unequal battle we were waging, and rejoiced at the wounds inflicted on our national pride. This makes no difference to us.

To Europe we will say:

We care nothing for your indifference; pray continue to look on, for the spectacle is worth the trouble. We have been devastated, pillaged without mercy, burnt out of our homes, weighed down by a war indemnity beyond parallel. In spite of our disasters, our mutilated country remains without fear, and will soon arise, for from the cinders that cover her you will see spring up a nation greater than you have ever seen before, and one strong enough to avenge herself.

To Prussia, so proud of her victories, we give the recommendation to think over the memories of her past history. Let her remember 1806, when we were prepared for the fray. She will see her armies routed and scattered between two sunsets; Berlin opening her gates at the very commencement of the campaign; Stettin and Magdeburg giving in without a struggle; the same sort of thing at Spandau, Lübeck, and other places; and, last of all, Blücher saving his army by a lie. To these instances of weakness we bring forward in answer the energy displayed at Belfort, Toul, Strasbourg, Metz, Verdun, and Paris, affording the world the mighty spectacle of a capital unwilling to yield to aught but famine. We have therefore good cause to hold up our heads in the presence of those whom we defeated at Jena and Auerstadt, for we fought one against three; at Froeschwiller one against four; and, as Prussia has imposed hard conditions on us and abused her triumph, let her reperuse her history and learn from it the lesson that awaits her when the ardently desired day shall arrive that we shall meet on the field of battle in equal numbers.

Let us then prepare, all aiding in the work without jealousy, and with a generous emulation. Let us acquire by industry the qualities that we stand in need of, and let us unite to rebuild the ruined edifice. After the dreadful disasters that France has undergone, our hearts can have but one thought, one ambition that of restoring and avenging our country, which has been so cruelly humbled.

Let us then take for a motto, *Courage and confidence in the future*, for it will most certainly give us a splendid revenge.

Cavalry at Vionville
&
Mars-la-Tour

Otto August Johannes Kaehler

German Cavalry at Vionville

Never since the battles of the Napoleonic wars has it been the lot of cavalry to act in larger bodies and play a more important role than in the conflicts around Vionville and Mars-la-Tour. In connection with the experiences of the campaign of 1870-71, in the use of large, independent bodies of cavalry in the service of security and information, the day of Vionville and Mars-la-Tour completes the picture by presenting its use in battle. In order to draw its lines sharply and mark its shades with all their peculiarities, it is requisite that the action of every participating link in the chain of events be represented as accurately as possible; only then may lessons be deduced from the facts for the future, and from them rules for the employment and leading of cavalry in battle.

In the following account of the cavalry conflicts at Vionville and Mars-la-Tour it has been the endeavour to draw such an accurate and complete picture of the conflicts. Although the official Prussian sources, as well as the French reports so far as they have reached the public, have been consulted, still the description cannot be free from gaps and distortions. It is given to the public for the purpose of affording an opportunity to all participants to contribute toward filling the gaps, straightening the facts, and completing the picture; the ampler the contributions, the better the interests of this matter will be subserved.

The 13th Brigade of the 5th Prussian Cavalry Division had come in touch with the French cavalry at Mars-la-Tour on the forenoon of August 15, 1870.[1]

---

1. 5th Cavalry Division: Commander, Lieutenant-General von Rheinbaben. General Staff Officer, Captain von Heister of the 10th Hussars.—11th Brigade: Major-General von Barby, 4th Cuirassiers, 13th Ulans, 19th Dragoons.—12th Brigade: Major-General von Bredow, 7th Cuirassiers, 16th Ulans, 13th Dragoons. (cont. next page)

During the afternoon the entire division had gone into bivouac, the 11th Brigade at Puxieux and Xonville, [2] the 12th to the east of Hannonville, the 13th to the east of Sponville. Of the two horse batteries present with the division, Bode's battery was with the 12th, Schirmer's battery with the 13th Brigade.

Outposts and patrols had observed the development of strong hostile corps of all arms on the *plateau* east of Vionville, on both sides of the *chaussée* to Metz. Clear insight into the strength and position of the hostile corps had not been gained.

Lieutenant-General von Rheinbaben reported the results gained by the troops under his command to the commander of the 10th Corps. The latter deemed further intelligence desirable and directed the general to advance against the enemy's position as early as possible on the 16th, in order to gain, by force if necessary, a closer view of the same. He at the same time promised a reinforcement of artillery.

Lieutenant-Colonel von Caprivi,[3] chief of staff of the 10th Corps, brought this reinforcement from Thiaucourt early on the morning of the 16th, consisting of the 1st and 3rd Horse Batteries of the 10th Field Artillery Regiment, escorted by the 2nd squadron of the 2nd Dragoons of the Guard.

The four horse batteries now with the division were placed under the command of Major von Koerber, of the 10th Field Artillery Regiment.

Lieutenant-General von Rheinbaben considered himself sufficiently strong to proceed to the execution of his task at 8:30 a. m.

The 13th Brigade, which had left its bivouac at Sponville at 6 a.m. and stood in readiness on the height to the west of the bottom of Puxieux, was ordered to escort the four batteries.

The 12th Brigade, likewise ready to march since daybreak, was directed to proceed from its bivouac near Hannonville to Mars-la-Tour and Vionville, and to take a position to the north of the *chaussée* suitable for covering the left flank of the artillery, which was also advanced to this place, as well as for joining in a further advance against the enemy's position.

—13th Brigade: Major-General von Redern, 10th Hussars, 11th Hussars, 17th Hussars.—1st Horse Battery, Capt. Bode I., of the 4th Artillery Regiment.—2nd Horse Battery, Capt. Schirmer, of the 10th Artillery Regiment. Total, 5,400 Horses, 12 Guns.

2. Xonville, Sponville, and Hannonville were, in a general direction, west of Puxieux and Chambley. Thiaucourt was some distance to the south.

3. Afterwards the Chancellor of the German Empire.—A. L. W.

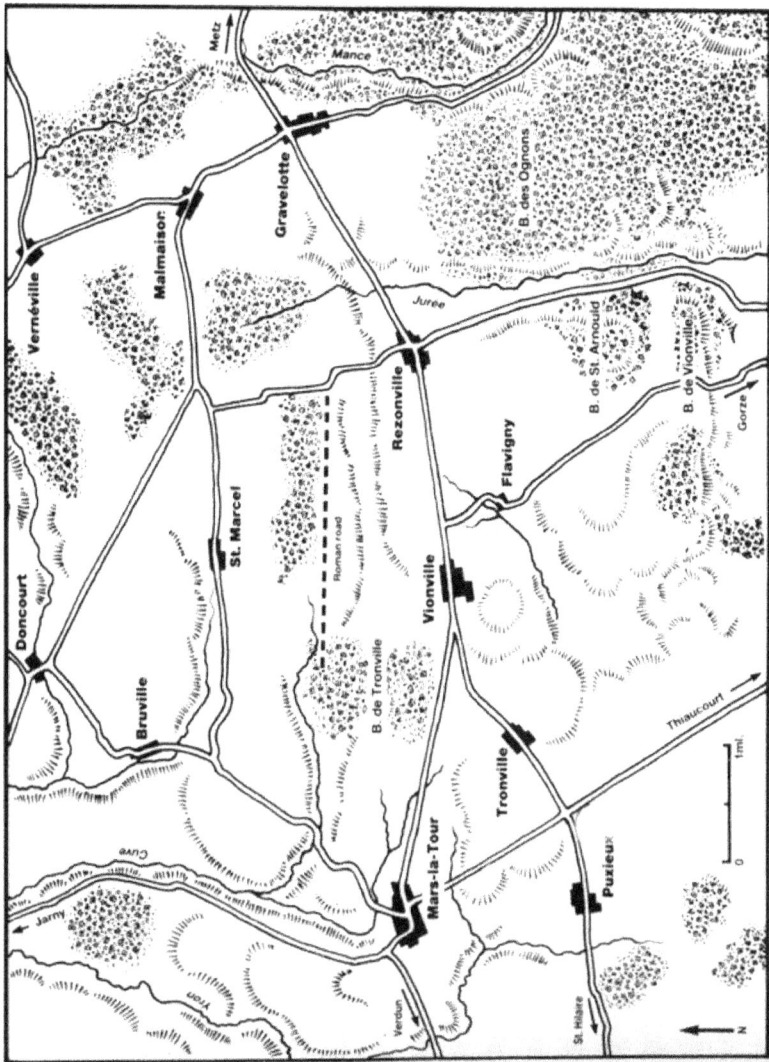

VIONVILLE—
MARS-LA-TOUR

Such a position was found in the bottom which extends from Vionville in a north-northwesterly direction toward Bruville; the brigade reached it at 9 a. m., finding there cover from the view and (for the present) also from the fire of the enemy. The latter was kept under observation by scouts. The brigade was drawn up in two lines of squadrons in closed line of platoon columns; in the first line on the right the 7th Cuirassiers, on the left the 16th Ulans, in second line three squadrons of the 13th Dragoons.[4]

The four horse batteries under command of Major von Koerber, escorted by the 13th Brigade and the 2nd squadron of the 2nd Guard Dragoons, had meanwhile trotted forward from the bottom on the west of Puxieux in the following order: Three squadrons of the 10th Hussars[5] and the 2-10 horse battery, Schirmer's, formed the advance guard, followed at the proper distance by the brigade in closed line of squadrons in platoon columns, with considerable intervals between regiments, on the right the 11th Hussars, on the left three squadrons of the 17th Hussars,[6] to which the 2nd squadron of the 2nd Guard Dragoons had attached itself. In rear of these regiments followed Horse Batteries 1-9, 1-10, and 3-10.

They moved at a lively trot in the general direction of Vionville, past Puxieux and beyond Tronville. On reaching the high ground near the latter place, the heads of Prussian infantry and cavalry detachments became visible to the south as they were descending from the heights near Chambley. It was the 6th Infantry Division.

On the part of the 13th Brigade, the 10th Hussars advanced in the ravine which stretches with various windings toward Gorze, to the point of its junction with the ravine coming from Flavigny, pushed scouts to the heights on the south, and thus covered the right flank. Schirmer's battery came in position at a gallop on the height east of Tronville, and opened fire immediately on a cavalry camp visible near Vionville.

The remaining three horse batteries soon came up and formed on the left of Schirmer's battery as they arrived, extending as far as the *chaussée* Tronville—Vionville. The 11th Hussars took position in the

---

4. The 4th squadron of the regiment had been detached to Fleury on the east bank of the Moselle.

5. The 1st squadron had been detached to establish communication with the 3rd Army.

6. Soon after 6 a. m. the 3rd squadron had been despatched to Maizeray on the Verdun *chaussée* to reconnoitre on the left flank; it was recalled at 11:30 a. m., but after its return the regiment was engaged in no further conflicts on that day.

ravine in rear of the right flank of the artillery position, the 17th Hussars and the 2nd squadron of the 2nd Dragoons of the Guard in rear of the left flank, to the north of, and close to, Tronville.

The first shells of Schirmer's battery threw the troops of Murat's Dragoon Brigade of de Forton's Cavalry Division,[7] which were just about to ride their horses to water as though they were many miles from the enemy, in the utmost confusion and disordered flight.

A French account gives the following description:

General de Forton's cavalry was to march off at 5 a. m., but counter-orders were issued, and at 9 a. m. the troops unsaddled and unbridled. The dragoon officer on outpost twice reported the approach of a numerous cavalry and artillery; a general staff officer was sent to investigate. He reported that nothing could be seen to give anxiety, and orders were given that three squadrons of each regiment should ride to water, while the fourth should be kept in readiness for an emergency.

Water had barely been reached when the first Prussian shells came hissing through the village and bivouacs. Informed by their scouts of our carelessness, the Prussian artillery had advanced at a gallop, come in position on both sides of the road, and fired with all its might

What a panic that was in the streets of Vionville! The men jumped on their horses and rushed into the streets, in which wagons and loose horses crowded and jammed. Disregarding the missiles which were flying about them, the officers endeavoured to stop their men, but succeeded only after considerable trouble in rallying a few platoons as a support on which the rest might rally, and thus they reached the *plateau* of Rézonville.

The *Cuirassier* Brigade (de Gramont), which on the previous evening had unfortunately left its first position and gone into bivouac farther to the rear, escaped this hail of canister, mounted in good order, and, to avoid being cut off by a strong column of hostile cavalry which threatened its right flank,[8] retired into the wood which skirts the Roman road eastward; passing by

---

7. 3rd Division of reserve cavalry: General de Forton. Chief of Staff, Colonel Durand de Villiers.—1st brigade: General, Prince Murat, 1st Dragoons, 9th Dragoons.—2nd brigade: General de Gramont, 7th Cuirassiers, 10th Cuirassiers, 7th and 8th batteries of the 20th Horse Artillery regiment.—Total, 1,600 horses, 12 guns.

8. This column must have been the 12th Cavalry Brigade.

Villers aux Bois, it debouched subsequently on the *plateau* of Rézonville to the right of the 9th Dragoons.

De Valabrègue's Division,[9] which had been on its guard and had quickly mounted, arrived soon afterward at the wood of Villers, in order not to serve uselessly as a target for the hostile artillery.

So far the French account.

One French squadron endeavoured to advance in closed formation to the north of the village, but was unable to withstand the fire from the Prussian guns, and hastily followed its fleeing comrades.[10] A hostile battery, which attempted to come in position in the same place, fared no better.

The Prussian cavalry subsequently reached the ground of the French bivouacs. All the headgear of the dragoons had been abandoned there; the cooking-pots were full of cooked food; wagons of all kinds, from the elegant carriages of the generals to the military chest, kitchen, and medicine wagons; a long table, all set, had to be abandoned at the moment when breakfast was ready to be served. Everything indicated the most complete surprise, the most hurried, disorderly flight.

The three Prussian batteries which came in position a little after Schirmer's battery could hardly open fire before they were led forward in line by Major von Koerber to the ridge immediately to the west of Vionville, on which the *chaussées* coming from Mars-la-Tour and Tronville meet.

Here they soon had occasion to direct their fire on the approaching hostile infantry and artillery, and to hold out to the end of the day in a glorious and changeable, but very unequal, contest.

At the same time Schirmer's battery advanced to the ridge which begins between Vionville and Flavigny and stretches away to the west, and took a most effective part in the conflicts around Vionville and Flavigny.

The 1st squadron of the 17th Hussars and the 2nd squadron of the 2nd Dragoons of the Guard escorted the batteries of Major von Koerber to their new position close to the west of Vionville and suffered

---

9. Cavalry division of the second corps: General de Valabrègue. Chief of Staff, Colonel de Cools. 1st brigade: General de Valabrègue, 4th Chasseurs, 5th Chasseurs.—2nd brigade: General Bachelier, 7th Dragoons, 12th Dragoons. Total, 1,800 horses.
10. Probably one of the squadrons which, according to the French account, had remained saddled and ready.

not inconsiderable losses, although they found some cover, among the rows of trees lining the Mars-la-Tour and Tronville *chaussées*, from the French projectiles, which began to fall with increasing frequency.

The 10th Hussars accompanied Schirmer's battery in its advance on the right and took position to the east of the road Vionville—La Beauville[11] at the point where it crosses the ravine which extends from Flavigny south-westward (bottom of Flavigny). The 11th Hussars also proceeded to this point upon orders from Lieutenant-General von Rheinbaben, but were soon recalled, about 10 a. m., by the brigade commander, Major-General von Redern, and dispatched to Tronville, where they were joined by two squadrons (2nd and 4th) of the 17th Hussars.

While these events were taking place, the 11th Brigade, which had been alarmed in its bivouac at Xonville soon after 8 a. m., received orders at 9 30 a. m. to follow the 13th Brigade; it was joined on the march near Puxieux by the 19th Dragoons, who had bivouacked here, and by the outposts furnished by this regiment, and took position to the southwest of Tronville at the place designated as rendezvous for the whole division, at a time when Major von Koerber's batteries were already in their second position; *i. e.,* after 10 a. m.

Soon after its arrival the brigade received orders from the division commander, Lieutenant-General von Rheinbaben, to take a more forward position to cover the left flank of the 13th Brigade. It advanced to the heights northeast of Tronville, where it received so vehement and effective a fire from hostile batteries which had meanwhile come in position to the northeast of Vionville, that the brigade commander, Major-General von Barby, was compelled to lead it to a more protected position in rear of the Tronville copses northwest of Vionville. This measure was all the more not only justified, but necessary for the safety of his troops, as Major-General von Barby, who had in person proceeded to the front to ascertain the situation, could discern neither danger to the 13th Brigade and the batteries entrusted to its protection, nor any objective of attack for his own brigade.

While these events were taking place with the 5th Cavalry Division, the 6th[12] had arrived on the battlefield.

---

11. La Beauville is the farm marked on the map west of Gorze. The road mentioned runs almost north and south.

12. 6th Cavalry Division: Commander, Major-General Duke William of Mecklenburg-Schwerin. General Staff Officer, Major von Schoenfels.—14th Brigade: Major-General von Grüter, 6th Cuirassiers, 3rd Ulans, 15th Ulans.—10th Brigade: Major-General von Rauch, 3rd Hussars, 16th Hussars, 2nd Horse Battery, Captain Wittstock. 3rd Art. Regt.—Total, 3,000 horses, 6 guns.

On the afternoon of the 15th of August this division had been ordered into cantonments around Coine sur Seille, on the right bank of the Moselle, by the commander of the 3rd Army Corps; at 2 a. m. on the 16th it had received orders from the same source "to be across the Moselle not later than 5:30 a. m., advance from Gorze toward the road Metz—Verdun, and take position on the *plateau* of Vionville, front toward Metz."

Notwithstanding that the division was at once alarmed, the 15th Brigade alone stood in readiness to advance on the left bank at 7 a. m., the suspension (chain) bridge at Novéant being passable only at a walk and in single file, on account of its considerable oscillation.

The general staff officer of the division, Major von Schoenfels, arrived at 7:30 a. m. at Gorze with the 3rd Hussars, who had been the first to cross; in rear of this regiment came the 16th Hussars, so far as they had been formed; in their rear and at a greater distance, Witt stock's battery; and lastly, the 14th Brigade, numbering but 10 squadrons, the 1st and 2nd squadrons of the 3rd Ulans having been left in the position between the Moselle and the Seille.

Major von Schoenfels trotted through Gorze with the 1st squadron of the 3rd Hussars, ascended to the southern edge of the height north of the village by the Vionville road, while the division was gradually assembling in rendezvous formation to the east of Gorze abreast of Chateau Catherine.

The squadron referred to soon reported "that strong columns of hostile infantry were marching on the *chaussée* from Gravelotte to Vionville and occupying the woods to the south of that road."

The regimental commander, Colonel von Zieten, now moved forward with the remaining three squadrons, advanced on the *plateau*, and pushed his scouts to the point where the roads to Vionville and Flavigny separate. They not only confirmed the former report, but also discovered a large body of hostile infantry, numbering several regiments, in a position of readiness on the north-western edge of the wood of Vionville.

While these observations were being communicated to the 5th Infantry Division now approaching from Gorze, Major-General von Rauch received orders to let the 16th Hussars follow the 3rd Hussars, and to advance with his brigade toward Rézonville. To support this movement and protect the infantry detachments holding Gorze, Wittstock's battery took position on the height immediately to the . north of the village.

The 14th Brigade was now directed to advance in the direction of Buxières in order to anticipate there the enemy's retreat if possible, and establish communication with the 5th Cavalry Division, of whose whereabouts and doings nothing specific was known. The opinion prevailed that the enemy was in full retreat on Verdun, and that the troops in front were his last columns and must be delayed and harassed as much as possible.

The 10th Brigade advancing in line of squadrons in platoon columns with deploying intervals, one squadron deployed in front to reconnoitre, immediately received from the westerly projecting corner of the wood of Vionville such vehement infantry fire that it was compelled not only to give up the advance, but to quit the *plateau* altogether and withdraw to the ravine northwest of Gorze, where it remained for the present. The brigade took up a position on both sides of the road Gorze—Vionville, the 16th Hussars on the right, the 3rd Hussars on the left.

The 14th Brigade, the 15th Ulans leading, did not long pursue its original direction on Buxières, but turned off to the north toward Vionville, because Lieutenant-General von Buddenbrock, commanding the 6th Infantry Division, which was about to debouch on Buxières, wished to have the *plateau* of Vionville reconnoitred before allowing his infantry to set foot upon it.

This movement of the 14th Brigade corresponded exactly to an order received at this time from the commanding general of the 3rd Corps, which required the entire division to advance on Vionville and to detach at least one regiment in the direction of Metz for the purpose of menacing the retreating enemy.

The concluding part of this order might have been easily carried out from the valley of the Moselle, but was now impracticable, since the troops were more than a mile from there and in the presence of a very strong and (as it appeared) greatly superior enemy; it was therefore not carried out.

The brigade advanced through the wood of Gaumont in the direction of Flavigny, and, on reaching the *plateau*, was joined by Wittstock's battery, which the division commander brought up from Gorze; it ascended the steep slope to the south of Flavigny (the 15th Ulans in first line, in second line and overlapping, the 6th Cuirassiers on the right, the two squadrons of the 3rd Ulans on the left), pushed back the hostile scouts without difficulty, and brought its battery into action to the east of the road Tronville—Gorze, near its point of crossing with the Chambley—Rézonville road, against large bodies of hostile infantry, which were advancing against Flavigny and the wood of Vionville. That portion of the infantry which advanced over the more open part of the *plateau* was hurriedly driven back by the shells of the battery; another portion, however, favoured by a depression of the ground, continued to advance, opened a severe fire on the battery, and compelled it to withdraw in rear of the brigade; the latter was in position on the edge of the bottom, and afterward, when the fire of the enemy's batteries made itself more and more felt, it descended into the depression north of the Chambley—Rézonville road.

Major von Koerber's batteries at Vionville had opened fire simultaneously with Wittstock's battery.

It was past 9 a. m.

Alarmed by the flight of its dragoons and by the fire of the Prussian batteries, the French infantry in its camps at Rézonville (6th and parts of 2nd Corps) had rapidly formed under arms; it advanced, simultaneously with the detachments farther to the south which had moved out as far as the wood of Vionville, against the Prussian cavalry divisions which, extending in a wide arc, held the southern and western edges of the *plateau*. Very soon afterward the French batteries opened fire, particularly from the northeast, against the Prussian guns at Vionville. The hostile infantry occupied Vionville, and soon afterward Flavigny also. Before its fire the batteries of Major von Koerber had to withdraw a short distance; the 1st Horse Battery (Bode's) of the 4th Regiment alone was able, partly covered as it was by the rows of trees lining the roads, to hold out at the junction point of the roads from Mars-la-Tour and Tronville.

The French shells also began more and more to search the ranks of the 12th Brigade (Major-General von Bredow's), which was posted in the bottom north of Vionville and now withdrew through the copses of Tronville, taking post to the right of the 11th Brigade, which had reached this point some time before.

Of the 13th Brigade, the 10th Hussars, from its position in the bottom of Flavigny, had dispatched its 3rd squadron to the height south of its position and east of the La Beauville—Vionville road, to protect batteries of the 3rd Corps, which off and on came in action there without escort. Giving way before the hostile infantry fire from Flavigny in the same measure as Von Koerber's batteries receded before it, the two other squadrons of the regiment had reached the junction point of the ravines which come down from Tronville and the farmstead of Sauley. Here the 3rd squadron rejoined, having been relieved from its escort duty by other cavalry (12th Dragoons).

After the 11th Hussars had been joined at Tronville, as above stated (mentioned earlier in this chapter),by two squadrons of the 17th Hussars, the brigade commander led them forward in platoon column, the 11th Hussars leading, in a north-easterly direction toward Vionville, for the purpose of joining the 12th Brigade and acting against the right flank of the hostile attack; but that brigade had just withdrawn through the copses of Tronville. The regiments of Major-General von Redern were likewise compelled to seek a position less exposed to the enemy's fire, and found it between the *chaussée* Mars-la-Tour—Vionville and the southernmost part of the Tronville copses; there they dismounted.

Meanwhile the 5th Infantry Division, advancing from the south and southwest, the corps artillery of the 3rd Corps, which had come in action on the height to the southwest of Flavigny, and the 6th Infantry Division, which made gradual progress to the north and, south of the Mars-la-Tour—Vionville *chaussée*, succeeded in compelling the French infantry and artillery, particularly to the south of the Mars-la-Tour Vionville *chaussée*,, to fall back and withdraw from Vionville and Flavigny.

By this time it was 12 o'clock noon.

At the same time the 1st squadron of the 17th Hussars (First Lieutenant von Hantelmann) and the 2nd squadron of the 2nd Guard Dragoons (Captain Prince von Sayn-Wittgenstein), which, with the exception of a few changes, had maintained their position in support of the left flank of Major von Koerber's batteries, although suffering some losses from French shells, were ordered by Colonel von Voigts-Rhetz, chief of staff of the 3rd Corps, to charge the hostile infantry on its retreat from Vionville. But this infantry had still such *moral* and good order, that the two squadrons failed to reach it and had to withdraw with considerable loss. (The squadron of the Guard Dragoons lost half of its horses.)

The 10th Hussars had also been sent forward at the same time and for the same purpose by Lieutenant-General von Alvensleben, commanding the 3rd Corps, but were unable to effect anything in front, as the enemy had halted on the Vionville—Rézonville *chaussée*. The division commander, Lieutenant-General von Rheinbaben, now dispatched the regiment around the north of Vionville to try its luck against the enemy's right flank. But here the hostile artillery forbade any advance beyond Vionville; the regiment therefore took up a position of readiness to the north of the *chaussée*, and between it and the southernmost of the Tronville copses, on the ground lately occupied by the 13th Brigade.

This brigade had meanwhile received orders from the division commander, who was nearby, to move more to the right and seek a position on the right of the 6th Infantry Division suitable for maintaining communication with the other troops of the 3rd Corps engaged on the right, and between this corps and the 5th Cavalry Division. In execution of this order Major-General von Redern led his remaining squadrons[13] down into the bottom of Flavigny, passing around the heights of Vionville by the south, and up to the village itself and close to the infantry hotly engaged near it. To protect the squadrons to some extent from the violent fire of friend and foe, they were led up as close as possible to the burning buildings of the village.

On the march to this position the 11th Hussars were joined by their 1st squadron and by what was left of the 2nd squadron of the 2nd Guard Dragoons. Shortly after 11 a. m. the left of the French 2nd Corps (Frossard's) began to give way, say the French accounts.

The Prussian infantry had been gaining ground all along the line from the wood of Vionville in the south to Flavigny and Vionville, and northward as far as the old Roman road. At the time when the 2nd French Corps in its position south of the Rézonville Vionville *chaussée* began to give way before the onsets of the Prussians, more particularly on its left, the 6th French Corps (Canrobert's) not only held its own north of the *chaussée* on the ridge northwest of Rézonville, but began to advance its right shoulder, resting it on the woods north of the Roman road, while at the same time fresh hostile forces made themselves felt, for the present by artillery alone, from the direction of St. Marcel and Bruville.

To arrest the retrograde movement of his corps and restore the battle, General Frossard resolved to attempt to overthrow the Prussian infantry, and sent orders to his cavalry to act.

Of this cavalry the 3rd Lancers[14] stood in first line to the south-

---

13. 11th Hussars and 2 squadrons of the 17th Hussars.

14. This regiment belonged to the 2nd Brigade (De la Mortiere's) of Brahaut's Cavalry Division of the 5th Corps (De Failly's), and had been detached together with the 1st Brigade (Lapasset's) of the 2nd Infantry Division (De Labadie d'Aydrien's) to Saarguemines, whence it had retired to Metz after the combat of Forbach with the 2nd Corps (Frossard's).

west of Rézonville, between the *chaussée* to Vionville and the road to Chambley. At the first shots of the Prussian artillery Marshal Bazaine had sent the 1st and 3rd Brigades of the Cavalry Division of the Guard[15] down into the valley which descends in a southerly direction from Bagneux and passes between the woods of St. Arnould and Ognon at the point where the old Roman road descends into it.

The 2nd Brigade of this division had started at 6 a. m. and escorted the emperor as far as Doncourt.[16] There it was relieved by De Margueritte's (1st) brigade (1st and 3rd Chasseurs d'Afrique) of the 1st Reserve Cavalry Division (Du Barail's), and found opportunity, during a subsequent phase of the battle, to take part in it north of Mars-la-Tour.

De Forton's division had, as above stated, (earlier in the chapter), reassembled at Villers aux Bois after it had been driven from the vicinity of Vionville by the Prussian shells. It was now ordered to advance to the old Roman road and "*à charger des que l' occasion se présentera.*" It took position in the depression into which the old Roman road descends, north of height 311, where it was joined by the Cavalry Division of the 2nd Corps under the command of General de Valabrègue.

On the ground between Rézonville and Villers aux Bois[17] there was now available of French cavalry: the 3rd Lancers, and three divisions of two brigades each; or one regiment of lancers, four of *chasseurs*, four of dragoons, four of *cuirassiers*; total, thirteen regiments, numbering 5,000 horses after deducting the losses already suffered on this day.

On receipt of the order from General Frossard, General Desvaux directed General du Preuil to move with the *cuirassiers* of the Guard to the south of the *chaussée* and to the rear of the 3rd Lancers to support them. The movement was at once executed and the regiment posted parallel to the ridge and slightly behind the crest, covered from the enemy's fire.

A few moments later the formation was changed to a column with a front of two squadrons, the 5th squadron in reserve.

---

15. Cavalry Division of the Imperial Guard: General Desvaux. Chief of Staff, Colonel Galinier. 1st brigade: General Halna du Frétay, The Guides Regiment of the Guard, The *Chasseurs-à-Cheval* of the Guard.—2nd brigade: General de France, The regiment of Guard Lancers, The regiment of Guard Dragoons.—3rd brigade: General du Preuil, The regiment of Guard *Cuirassiers*, The regiment of Guard *Carbineers*.—Total, 3,000 horses.
16. Southeast of Jarny on the Etain—Gravelotte road.
17. On a front of 2,500 paces, distant from the battlefield proper 2,500 to 3,000 paces.

About 12:30 p. m. according to Prussian accounts, about 11:30 a.m. according to French accounts;[18]

.... the fire, which up to that time had been very brisk, dropped, and French skirmishers could at once be seen on the crest of the ridge as they retreated at the double and without order. They were closely followed by the Prussian batteries, which at once crowned the heights and sent their shells among the French cavalry. Two squadrons of the 3rd Lancers advanced, but, after traversing some distance, they turned about, because no objective had been assigned them for their charge.

General du Preuil sent word to General Desvaux that where he was everything was in full retreat, but at the same time he received orders to attack. At this time his troops were so far from the line of the enemy's infantry[19] that defeat was certain unless the infantry was first shaken by artillery. This objection was urged, but General Frossard replied: "Charge at once, or we all are lost." General du Preuil at once threw forward the first line, which started at a gallop. The second followed at a distance of 150 meters, but, as the gait seemed too rapid, the general ordered it shortened, and then repaired with his staff to its flank. Moving at full speed, the first line had gained much ground and left the second far behind; the Prussian skirmishers were rallying to form squares, a movement which interrupted their fire.

The charge reached effective range without much loss, when its career was checked by a multitude of obstacles strewn over the ground, consisting of biscuit boxes, baggage wagons, and camp equipments which the fleeing troops had thrown away in their hurry.

Cramped in its advance, the first line was obliged to oblique to the left, and the more they advanced the more the crowding caused by the oblique movement increased, and finally threw the two squadrons into disorder; at a range of 30 meters it was greeted with a terrible fire, and the whole line dispersed and poured into the defile formed by the Prussian squares. The lieutenant-colonel was seriously wounded; the commander, mortally hit, nevertheless broke into the square, followed by one adjutant, who was at once bayoneted. The rest, on retreating, were compelled to pass by the squares, received fire from four sides, and were annihilated.

---

18. This discrepancy of time may be readily reconciled in that the French may have noticed the wavering of their lines before it became apparent to their opponents.
19. The Prussian infantry had not yet passed much beyond Flavigny, and was therefore about 2,500 paces distant.

The second line was now unmasked; at a distance of 300 meters it was received with rapid fire, which knocked over some few men, but the advance was continued in good order, as the fire ceased for a moment; but when it had approached to within 100 meters, the command "*Chargez!*" was answered by the Prussians with a hail of canister and bullets which brought more than half of the line to the ground. The balance encountered obstacles of a permanent character, or fell into a ditch 10 meters in front of the squares.

The third line fared no better, and was dispersed by the fire like the others.

22 officers, 208 men, and 243 horses *hors de combat* represent the losses of the *cuirassiers*. As they had failed to shake ("*entamer*") the squares charged, the result was *nil*.

So far the French accounts. The Prussian narrative describes the event as follows :

This cavalry charge strikes in the first line the companies of the 10th Brigade, which were advancing eastward beyond Flavigny. The Second Battalion of the 52nd Infantry Regiment, under Captain Hildebrandt, awaits the charge in line with arms at a carry; at 250 paces a rapid fire begins, against which the enemy's blow shivers impotently. But other swarms of horsemen pass the little band on the right and left, the rear rank faces about and fires into the enemy from the rear.

On one side the fusilier companies of the 12th Infantry Regiment, and on the other the various companies of the 6th Infantry Division, which had advanced between the *chaussée* and Flavigny, receive the hostile horsemen with a fire as steady as it is destructive. Far and wide the field is covered with dead and wounded; only a small band of these *cuirassiers*, who charged with such superb courage, succeed in escaping destruction by hasty retreat.

The further events are described by French accounts[20] as follows:

To cover the rally of the defeated cuirassiers, Marshal Bazaine had sent a battery of the Guard to the line of battle,[21] and was among the guns with his staff, attentively observing the retreat of his horsemen, who had now arrived abreast of his position,

---

20. Fay, page 81.
21. To the northern slope of cone 311, southwest of Rézonville and north of the road to Chambley.

when all of a sudden Prussian hussars were discovered among them, and immediately afterward also among the guns, no one having noticed their approach before.

Let us see how these Prussian hussars got there.

Lieutenant-Colonel von Caprivi, the chief of staff of the 10th Corps, had observed the approach of the French *cuirassiers* from his position on the height of Flavigny, and called the attention of Major-General von Redern, who stood there in readiness with part of his brigade.[22] to this favourable opportunity for action. The 17th Hussars, posted on the left, at once trotted forward in line of platoon columns, accompanied on the left by the 2nd squadron of the 2nd Guard Dragoons, passed around the north of the wet meadows lying east of Flavigny, through the midst of the infantry, which greeted them with a loud hurrah, formed line, and cut in among the now retreating French *cuirassiers*.

During further pursuit of the same toward Rézonville the regimental commander, Lieutenant-Colonel von Rauch, noticed the French battery above mentioned and galloped toward it, followed by some twenty hussars. The surprise was so complete that the guns could not be limbered up. They were laid on the approaching hussars and fired at a range of 80 meters, but failed to stop the charge a moment. The cannoneers defended themselves and were almost all cut down. Some teams, whose drivers had been killed, stood there quietly, and the hussars made an attempt to remove the guns with their aid, but were prevented by hostile cavalry.

Some hussars (according to French accounts, notably an officer) threw themselves on Marshal Bazaine, who was in the midst of the battery and tried to escape by beating a hasty retreat, the officers of his staff being compelled to draw their swords in defence, as the marshal's escort squadrons had been left behind at Rézonville. General du Preuil, perceiving the marshal's danger, called up these escort squadrons, one of the 5th Hussars,[23] and one of the 4th Chasseurs à Cheval.[24] Their appearance prevented the hussars from removing the guns

---

22. 11th Hussars, 3 squadrons of the 17th Hussars, 2nd squadron of the 2nd Guard Dragoons.

23. Of the 1st Brigade (De Berni's) of the Cavalry Division of the 5th Corps (De Failly's), which had probably joined the army at Metz with Lapasset's Brigade. Compare footnote 14.

24. Of the 1st Brigade (De Valabrègue's) of the Cavalry Division of the 2nd Corps (Frossard's).

and compelled them to retreat, as well as the 2nd and 4th squadrons of their regiment, which had charged more to the left against the *chaussée* Vionville—Rézonville and had come under a very effective fire from hostile infantry.

The 11th Hussars, checked by the marshy meadows east of Flavigny, which they had to cross, deployed somewhat later than the 17th Hussars. After passing through the Prussian infantry, they encountered, on ascending the western slope of height 311 south of Rézonville, disordered bands of French infantry and cavalry, which were for the most part ridden down or dispersed. The 1st squadron, under Captain von Vaerst, joined in the charge of the 17th Hussars on the battery of the French Guard above referred to.

A severe flank fire from the Rézonville—Vionville *chaussée*, and the retreat of the 17th Hussars, compelled the 11th Hussars, both being disordered by the long charge (2,500 paces on the air-line), to fall back to the Flavigny meadows. Here the regiment was assembled and, on being formed, withdrawn to the height west of the cemetery of Vionville, where it dismounted.

The 17th Hussars also assembled and re-formed south-west of Flavigny and remained halted in the bottom, where, soon after 1:30 p.m., they were joined by the 11th Hussars, called up by Major-General von Bedern, and subsequently by the 3rd squadron (detached to Maizeray; see footnote 6).

The losses of the 11th Hussars were: dead, 1 man, 8 horses; wounded, 1 officer, 18 men, 5 horses; missing, 2 men, 17 horses; total, 1 officer, 21 men, 30 horses.

The losses of the 17th Hussars were: dead, 8 men, 74 horses; wounded, 2 officers, 68 men; missing, 14 men; total, 2 officers, 90 men, 74 horses.

Of the 6th Cavalry Division we know that soon after 9 a, m. it was compelled by the increasing fire of the enemy to send the 14th Brigade and Wittstock's battery down into the ravine east of the wood of the Côte Fuzée, while the 15th Brigade took position in the valley north of St. Thiébault. The latter brigade soon received orders to close up on the 14th Brigade, and in execution of this order it marched by the ravine which stretches through the wood of Gaumont toward Tronville; it reached the road La Beauville—Vionville soon after 11 a.m., and took position there for the present.

Shortly after noon, at the time when the French 2nd Corps retreated, some portions in full flight, the 6th Cavalry Division received orders from Lieutenant-General von Alvensleben, commanding the 3rd Corps, "to advance on Rézonville, as the enemy's infantry was retreating in disorder."

Just before the receipt of this order the 15th Brigade had again been moved up on the *plateau*, with directions to join the right of the corps artillery of the 3rd Corps, which was in action there, with a view of acting from there concentrically with the 14th Brigade, which the division commander was contemplating to dispatch past Flavigny against Rézonville; for this reason the latter brigade was even now advancing.

As the 15th Brigade was about to advance from its position near the corps artillery in obedience to these directions, it was stopped by Lieutenant-General von Stülpnagel, commanding the 5th Infantry Division, "in order not to interfere with the field of fire of the artillery."

Concurrently with these movements of the 6th Cavalry Division, an advance all along the enemy's line became visible. It was therefore with a view to repel a threatened attack, not to pursue a retreating enemy, that the division commander now decided to advance with both brigades past Flavigny and direct his attack against the dense hostile masses advancing from Rézonville, at the very moment when the 13th Brigade, weakened by the length of the charge and the dispersion which was the inevitable consequence of the various personal encounters, was compelled to give way before the closed charge of Marshal Bazaine's escort squadrons.

The division advanced in line of squadrons in platoon columns with deploying intervals, and passed close to the south of the burning village of Flavigny, on the right the 15th Brigade, with the 3rd Hussars on the right and the 16th Hussars on the left; on the left and slightly held back in second line, as it were, the 14th Brigade, with the 15th Ulans leading, 3 squadrons of the 6th Cuirassiers on the left rear,[25] and 2 squadrons of the 3rd Ulans on the right rear, both overlapping the 15th Ulans.[26]

In passing the 15th Brigade touched the left flank of the 5th Infantry Division, which was hotly engaged, and traversed the former

---

25. The 4th squadron of the regiment remained with Wittstock's battery as special escort; the battery had ere this joined the corps artillery of the 3rd Corps, where it continued to take an effective part in the conflicts of the day.

26. The official map of the battle of Mars-la-Tour, situation at noon, shows the 3rd Ulans on the left and the 6th Cuirassiers on the right rear.—*Translator.*

positions of the French skirmish lines, which were outlined along a slight fold of the ground by a long and uninterrupted line of dead and wounded. The charge was not carried out as contemplated; no faster gait than a trot was taken, nor was line formed, since a crowding leftward which originated on the right had obliterated all the intervals, and the brigade was moving in a dense mass of squadrons in platoon columns. While in this unfavourable formation the brigade came under very brisk fire at close range from dense swarms of skirmishers ensconced in a fold of the terrain.

At the same moment Major-General von Rauch, one of the brigade commanders, was wounded and obliged to hand his command over to Colonel von Schmidt, of the 16th Hussars. The losses, which under the circumstances increased rapidly, and the certainty of failure, caused the colonel to arrest the movement. He gave the command to halt and restore the intervals between squadrons by a lateral movement; after a short halt, the squadrons were wheeled about by platoons and withdrawn at a walk, because the rest of the cavalry was also withdrawing and the present formation of the brigade (closed line of squadrons in platoon columns) was unsuited for action, since space was lacking for deployment.

The brigade now took deploying intervals at a walk under an uninterrupted, brisk fire from the hostile infantry and artillery, and then retired at a trot behind some copses on the edge of the ravine which stretches toward the farmstead of Sauley. These difficult movements, ordered with great calmness and deliberation, were carried out in excellent order.

Of the 3rd Hussars the colonel commanding (Von Zieten) and Lieutenants von Witzleben and von Byern were severely wounded; in re-forming 80 men and more than 100 horses were missing. The losses of the 16th Hussars were not quite so heavy, since it was chiefly the former regiment that had come under the enemy's infantry fire.

The 14th Brigade, which had to traverse 3,500 paces over hill and dale, strained every nerve to be in time, and come in at least for some gleaning. At the time when the regiment got beyond Flavigny, the larger mounted bodies of the enemy had already left the battlefield near Flavigny[27] and withdrawn under the protection of the infantry occupying Rézonville. Part of the 17th Hussars were coming straight against the *ulans* and passed through the intervals.

At the heels of the hussars, and before the *ulans* could deploy, a

27. The *cuirassiers* of the Guard, who had charged the Prussian infantry at Flavigny.

French hussar squadron[28] threw itself on the latter from the right front.[29] The 1st squadron (Captain Brix) moved to charge in flank, wheeled left into line, and, in company with the leading platoons of the other squadrons, threw the hostile squadron back with considerable loss. The regiment was then assembled and formed by the regimental commander, Lieutenant-Colonel von Alvensleben, within effective range of the enemy's infantry fire from Rézonville, on which occasion, as a matter of instruction for the young troops in their first charge, the formation and dressing were effected, front toward the enemy, the same as on the drill-ground. The brigade commander soon afterward gave orders for the return march, which was begun at a walk.

In the second line of the 14th Brigade, as previously mentioned, three squadrons of the 6th Cuirassiers advanced on the left, overlapping, in line of squadrons in platoon columns, at first without, afterward with deploying intervals, and, passing close to the burning village of Flavigny, formed line as soon as sufficient space was found. There was no longer any objective of attack, since the hostile infantry columns desisted, from the contemplated offensive blow, and their leading detachments, upon the approach of the Prussian cavalry, threw themselves hurriedly into the ditches of the Rézonville—Vionville *chaussée*, whence they opened an effective fire.

The two squadrons of the 3rd Ulans advanced in line of squadrons in platoon columns left in front, close in rear of the 15th Ulans and overlapping the latter's right. In passing the artillery in action south of Flavigny both squadrons had to oblique to the left, which brought them in rear of the right wing of the 15th Ulans; but when the left flank battery suspended its fire, they obliqued to the right again. Dispersed hostile horsemen of the enemy and many skirmish lines were visible.

The regimental commander, Colonel von der Groeben, selected the latter for his objective and had the "gallop" sounded. Suddenly the right flank squadron of the 15th Ulans wheeled to the left into line

---

28. Of the 5th Regiment and part of Marshal Bazaine's escort; it had saved the latter from capture by the 17th and 11th Hussars.

29. The regiment at this time must have been between the road Chambley Rézonville and the eastern extremity of the marshy meadow near Flavigny, for the 17th Hussars and the 5th French Hussars were coming from the Guard battery which Marshal Bazaine had ordered in action north of the road named and on height 311, and in which he came near being captured.

against the hostile cavalry[30] and masked the front of both squadrons of the 3rd Ulans just as they were in the act of forming line.

Only the 4th platoon of the 4th squadron, Captain von Hammerstein of this squadron, and all the platoon leaders, who had pushed through the 15th Ulans, were with their regimental commander in front of the regiment. When soon afterward the brigade commander ordered the retreat, the commander of the 3rd Ulans remained halted with the 4th platoon of his 4th squadron under a brisk infantry and artillery fire, assembled his two squadrons, and followed the other two regiments of the brigade only upon specific order, at a walk, and wheeling twice about and facing the enemy.

The 1st and 2nd squadrons, as well as three platoons of the 3rd squadron of the 9th Dragoons (the divisional cavalry of the 19th Infantry Division), had reached the battlefield from Novéant with the detachment of Colonel von Lynker; they were under command of Major von Studnitz,[31] and joined the 6th Cavalry Division at 9 a. m. in its position in the ravine Gorze Tronville, taking position on the right of the 15th Ulans.[32] They took part in the movement just described in the same relative position, and continued to act with this division.

In like manner the 1st and 2nd squadrons and two platoons of the 4th squadron of the 12th Dragoons,[33] which had been assigned to the 12th Infantry Division as divisional cavalry, joined in the movement of the 6th Cavalry Division to the left of the 16th Hussars and connecting their left with the right of the three squadrons of the 9th Dragoons.[34]

---

30. French hussar squadron of the 5th Regiment, escort of Marshal Bazaine.

31. The regimental staff, the 4th squadron, and one platoon of the 3rd squadron remained with the detachment; during the subsequent course of the battle they went wherever they hoped to find an opportunity, and succeeded repeatedly in taking an effective part.

32. The official map of the battle of Mars-la-Tour, at 12 o'clock noon, shows the 9th Dragoons to the right and 500 paces in front of the 15th Ulans.—*Translator.*

33. The 3rd squadron of the regiment had been detached to the right flank to join the second battalion of the Body Guard Regiment; two platoons of the 4th squadron to join the 10th Infantry Brigade.

34. The official map of the battle of Mars-la-Tour, at 12 o'clock noon, shows the 12th Dragoons 200 paces to the right and 400 paces to the front of the 9th Dragoons. According to the text, the 9th Dragoons and 12th Dragoons would have been in line abreast of each other and between the 14th and 15th Brigades, while the official map shows these brigades posted with an interval of about 100 paces only, and the 9th and 12th Dragoons, who could not possibly have found space in this interval, are shown a considerable distance in front. (Cont. next page.)

Both regiments came within the most effective fire, but not in contact with the enemy.

Although of all these regiments the 15th Ulans alone had partially succeeded in "cutting in," still the whole movement had not remained without some influence on the course of the battle. The hostile infantry desisted from its advance south-westward beyond the *chaussée* and returned to its rifle-trenches, the hostile cavalry disappeared entirely from this part of the battlefield and did not again appear south of Rézonville, the batteries to the north of the *chaussée* took a more rearward position, and the 5th and 6th Infantry Divisions escaped for the moment from a most serious situation.

In the course of the movement the regiments had traversed a distance of nearly 5,000 paces and back to the place of assembly, altogether more than a German mile.

The division remained in this place southwest of Flavigny until about 4 p. m., when the fire of a renewed hostile advance from the north (St. Marcel—Bruville) compelled it to retire to the great ravine Tronville—Gorze at its junction with the ravine coming down from the farmstead of Sauley.

While these things were happening around Flavigny and to the east of it between 11 a. m. and 1 p. m., the rest of the cavalry present on the battlefield had not been idle.

The 11th and 12th Brigades, as we know, sought and found shelter on the west of the Tronville copses from the hostile artillery fire, which became more and more vehement and effective. Soon afterward, about 11 a. m., the 13th Dragoons of the 12th Brigade, after being rejoined by the 4th squadron,[35] had been thrown forward toward St. Marcel and Bruville to height 277, where hostile bodies began to show themselves, particularly near the former place. Soon afterward hostile detachments of all arms began to appear at Bruville also, but disappeared again.

Meanwhile the 6th Infantry Division had come in action near Vionville with good result, but the whole 3rd Corps was now engaged from the wood of Vionville to the copses of Tronville north of the *chaussée*. In consequence the commanding general, Lieutenant-General von Alvensleben, made increased efforts to have some

---

In their position the 12th Dragoons could connect their left with the right of the 9th Dragoons, but it is not clear how they could have been on the left of the 16th Hussars. In this particular the author's sources were evidently defective.—*Translator.*

35. Detached to Fleury. See footnote 4.

reserves in hand for this long line, and to strengthen it as much as possible. For this purpose there were in the first place available two brigades (11th and 12th) of the 5th Cavalry Division, which, with this view, had been moved to Tronville about noon, taking position in the triangle between the *chaussées* Vionville—Tronville and Vionville—Mars-la-Tour, on the northern slopes of height 288. They were facing northeast; the 11th Brigade was on the right, the 12th on the left; the 13th Dragoons remained on the heights south of Bruville, and the last named brigade thus numbered but two regiments, the 7th Cuirassiers and 16th Ulans.

At this time the enemy was making renewed efforts to regain the lost ground. Marshal Canrobert, whose corps, as stated above, was engaged north of the *chaussée*, extended his right for the purpose of turning the Prussian left. An attack from St. Marcel by entirely fresh troops became also more imminent every minute. Despite all its efforts, the Prussian infantry failed to gain and hold any considerable ground beyond the line Flavigny—Vionville. The French batteries on the heights northeast of Rézonville rendered every advance nugatory; the 1st Division (Tixier's) of Canrobert's Corps, in the woods north of the Roman road, prevented any attempt against these batteries.

The commanding general of the 3rd Army Corps, Lieutenant-General von Alvensleben, perceived the necessity of terminating this state of affairs, as it threatened to become ruinous if allowed to develop further. He now ordered the three battalions of Colonel Lehmann into the Tronville copses[36] to meet the danger threatening from the north, and directed Lieutenant-General von Rheinbaben to send one of his brigades against the hostile advance between the Roman road and the great *chaussée*, and to detach another around the Tronville copses by the west to cooperate with Colonel Lehmann's detachment in covering the left of the 6th Infantry Division.

In pursuance to these arrangements, Colonel von Voigts-Rhetz, chief of staff of the 3rd Corps, rode up to Major-General von Bredow and asked him to comply with what had been agreed upon between Lieutenant-Generals von Alvensleben and von Rheinbaben, and to advance past the woods in front—pointing toward the Tronville copses—against the enemy's infantry and artillery. The colonel added that we had taken Vionville; that the hostile infantry between the wood

---

36. 3½ battalions, 1 battery of the 37th Infantry Brigade had been detached by the 10th Corps from Thiaucourt toward Chambley to cover the right flank of the corps, and had there taken part in the engagement of the 3rd Corps.

and the *chaussée* must be overthrown to render an advance of our infantry beyond the village practicable; also that by an early and vigorous attack the general could contribute materially toward a successful issue.

The task as stated was definite and left no doubt, nor did Major-General von Bredow hesitate to proceed to its vigorous execution. Believing the infantry which appeared in the Tronville copses before him to be hostile, he decided to send two squadrons there to cover the left flank of his charge. These squadrons were considered lost under any circumstances, and the lot was cast to determine which of the eight squadrons should sacrifice themselves for their comrades. The lot fell on the 3rd squadron of the 7th Cuirassiers and on the 1st squadron of the 16th Ulans. Their task, however, as events proved, was the less dangerous of the two, for, as we know, the copses were held by Prussian infantry, and although the squadrons came under the enemy's infantry fire, they suffered but little loss and formed afterward the nucleus around which the brigade rallied.

The remaining six squadrons of the brigade[37] advanced toward Vionville in closed line of squadrons in platoon columns, the *cuirassiers* leading, crossed west of Vionville to the north side of the *chaussée*, passed by the left of a Prussian battery in action there, changed direction half left, descended into the bottom which extends from the north of Vionville toward Bruville, and deployed to the right under effective artillery fire.

The 7th Cuirassiers were on the left, and had nine platoons in line and two in rear of the left;[38] the 16th Ulans were on the right, with all three squadrons in line and slightly in rear as a sort of second line. In this formation the brigade made a slight wheel to the half right and advanced at a gallop against the hostile batteries in action on the western edge of the ridge northwest of Rézonville.

As the 12th Brigade descended into the bottom to form for the charge, Major von Koerber, who during the previous conflicts had held his four horse batteries to their position west of Vionville, concentrated the fire of all his guns on the position of the enemy's artillery, and thus prepared the charge in an effective manner by facilitating the advance of the regiments. As the charge got under way, he accompanied it with a few rounds, which he fired against the enemy

---

37. 1st, 2nd, and 4th of the 7th Cuirassiers, and 2nd, 3rd, and 4th of the 16th Ulans.
38. The first platoon of the 1st squadron was detached on relay service and did not rejoin the regiment until after the end of the combat.

obliquely across the right flank of the regiments—right before their feet, as it were.

This artillery fire engaged the enemy's attention so completely that the 12th Brigade succeeded in traversing the distance of 1,500 paces to the nearest batteries of the enemy without much loss, and in surprising them in headlong charge.

But let the regiments tell their own stories.

Major Count von Schmettow, commanding the 7th Cuirassiers.[39] says:

> We penetrated into the first battery, of which but two guns succeeded in firing. The battery commander and all the men were cut down. Conscious of the prime necessity of overthrowing as many of the enemy as possible between the wood and *chaussée*, the regiment, under a flanking infantry fire from the wood, threw itself upon a second battery and an infantry column. Whatever of this battery did not reach the shelter of its infantry was cut down.
>
> According to the instructions given by Major-General von Bredow, we were not to stop at the first line to make prisoners, but to charge the second line at once. In execution of these instructions the regiment cut down and stabbed everything within reach. Arriving thus at the foot of the elevation which marked the enemy's main position,[40] two squadrons of hostile *cuirassiers*[41] suddenly assailed the regiment in rear, which now had every avenue of escape cut off except on the right. In selecting this route we retreated pell-mell with the French cuirassiers, who attacked with little energy, and some of whom accompanied us on their runaway horses to the rear of our infantry, where they were cut down.

The 16th Ulans state:

> The hostile battery, whose left wing we struck, was traversed. Men and horses were for the most part cut down, so that the guns were reduced to silence. In rear of this battery the regi-

---

39. The commander of the regiment Lieutenant-Colonel von Larisch, had his arm broken by a fall of his horse while marching through the Palatinate, and had to remain behind.

40. Western slope of height 311 north of Rézonville.

41. Of the 7th Cuirassiers of the 2nd Brigade (De Gramont's) of the 3rd (De Forton's) Reserve Cavalry Division.

ment struck another, and, more toward the *chaussée*, infantry squares also, which were posted on a hill, and rode down the two on the right almost completely and dispersed the others for the most part.

The enemy's fire, and the long distance and the exhaustion of the horses, had thrown the squadrons into disorder, and the officers, being unable to make themselves heard above the din of the battle, were powerless to hold back the men, who were riding onward with terrible fury, so that the attack proceeded irresistibly and struck the second line of the enemy's infantry on the heights near Rézonville, while at the same time hostile cavalry came trotting forward from the bottom of Rézonville and from the old Roman road, on our right hussars[42] and *chasseurs*,[43] on our left *cuirassiers*[44]

This new enemy was not at once perceived, because at this moment a *mitrailleuse* battery, which had been posted in rear of the first line of infantry and was in the act of escaping, had been overtaken and everybody was busily engaged in cutting down the drivers. The men in front were thrown back, carrying those nearest with them, all turned about, and now we went back, for the most part the way we had come, on winded horses, in a dense crowd, *ulans*, *cuirassiers*, hussars, *chasseurs*, hostile *cuirassiers*, dispersed infantry men, cutting, stabbing, firing, between and over standing and overthrown guns and limbers, past the infantry which had reassembled in knots, past the front of the hostile *cuirassiers*, under a murderous hail of shells and rifle bullets, to the rear of the Prussian batteries posted north of Vionville, where some infantry protected the remnants of the regiment and brigade.

Fortunately, the hostile cavalry pursued with little determination, and their skirmishers, which (particularly those of the *cuirassiers*) restricted themselves to the use of their firearms, were soon recalled by the trumpet. The remnants of the regiment withdrew by the bottom extending toward Flavigny, where they had the joy of finding the regimental standard, which the

---

42. This must be an error; there were no French hussars on this part of the battlefield, except Marshal Bazaine's escort squadron of the 5th Regiment, which, according to French accounts, took no part in this conflict.

43. Division de Valabrègue.

44. 2nd Brigade (de Gramont's) of De Forton's (3rd) Cavalry Division.

devotion and bravery of four non-commissioned officers and ten *ulans*[45] had barely succeeded in saving.

Let us hear what impression this Prussian charge made on the opponent. Lieutenant-Colonel Fay writes:

"They"—the Prussian *cuirassiers* and *ulans*—"threw themselves bravely against the position,"—of the French batteries—"penetrated our lines, and when they reached the height which conceals De Forton's Division from them, we see them coming down along the woods south of Villiers as fast as their horses will carry them. The opportunity for our cavalry is too good; it is put in motion at once with sabres drawn, our Dragoon Brigade,[46] and soon afterward the 7th Cuirassiers, throw themselves on these masses, which are surprised by the unexpected encounter; two squadrons of the *cuirassiers* assail from the rear, and throw them in complete disorder after inflicting considerable loss."

Lieutenant-Colonel Bonie says:

"After he"—the enemy—"had begun to silence our guns by the fire of his own,[47] he throws forward two *échelons* of cavalry with 100 meters distance, the *cuirassiers* in first line, the *ulans* in second. This column approaches at the charging gallop, breaks through our foot *chasseurs*, sabres the batteries, and seeks to retreat when arrived in rear of the last line of our infantry. But the enemy has been unaware of the presence of our cavalry, which now surprises and annihilates him."

We have recounted above, in consequence of what movements the divisions of De Forton and De Valabrègue had taken position near the wood which skirts the Roman road. On arriving there, the two brigades of General de Forton had formed column of regiments, right in front, and subsequently made several changes of front in order to face toward Rézonville or Vionville, according to circumstances. After its last movement, the 2nd Brigade[48] were in inversion, the regiments in brigade as well as the squadrons in the regiment. In this formation

---

45. These brave men were Sergeant Gaebler, standard-bearer, Sergeant Hause, the non-commissioned officers Prange and Hoppe (the latter falling a victim of his devotion), Lance Corporal Grosch, and the *ulans* Luhmann, Vogel, Zunder, Menger, Solle, and Mewes. The names of the other three could not be ascertained.

46. Murat's Brigade (1st) of the 3rd (De Forton's) Reserve Cavalry Division.

47. The batteries of Major von Koerber.

48. De Gramont's, 7th and 10th Cuirassiers.

CHARGE OF BREDOW'S BRIGADE.

German Cavalry ▨ Infantry ▥

French do ▢ do ▪

Contours at intervals of 30 feet.

VON BREDOW'S CHARGE

the brigade was led forward to the *plateau*, its rear resting on the wood, close to the Roman road.

After the hostile horsemen had traversed our batteries, General de Forton charged them with his dragoons and part of his *cuirassiers*. They advanced with deployed regiments and threw themselves on the approaching lines. At the collision the 9th Dragoons broke through the Prussian *cuirassiers*, who readily opened their ranks and turned to the right and left in order to retreat to the position of our artillery and rejoin the *ulans* which had already passed them in retreat. At the end of their charge, the latter had turned about in order to retreat, but were even then assailed by the remaining squadrons of our *cuirassiers* at the mere call '*Attention, les cuirassiers! Partez!*'

As this call failed to designate any formation, the advance was made in disorderly crowds; the officers had to put their horses to their best speed in order to remain at the head of their men, who were going full tilt. A terrible confusion resulted; the 16th Ulans, taken in flank and overthrown, were cut down and briskly pursued until the white column of the *cuirassiers* approached and rescued them. In consequence of the long distance covered at a gallop, the horses were completely blown and at the end of their strength. At this moment the horsemen of De Valabrègue's Division, joining those of General de Forton, threw themselves upon the enemy; everything became intermixed as in a tornado, and both sides fought with frenzy.

The fury of our men was so great, everyone was so much engaged with his opponent, that the slaughter continued although the rally was sounded. In a few moments the hostile cavalry was destroyed, the ground covered with the bodies of the *ulans* and white iron-clad riders. Those alone who had the best mounts or were made prisoners escaped the slaughter. At this time the infantry from Vionville began to cover the ground where the 7th Cuirassiers were fighting with a severe fire, the recall was again sounded, and our regiments were re-formed (*reformés*) and withdrawn to the bottom of Gravelotte.

Borne along by a five-fold[49] superior hostile cavalry, which was

---

49. According to French reports, the following rode against the 12th Brigade at the end of its charge: the divisions of De Forton and De Valabregue, each four regiments strong according to the order of battle above given. Even considering that the French regiments were weak and numbered no more (cont. next page),

perfectly fresh and attacked almost from a halt, fired into during retreat by the remnants of the hostile infantry, the greater part of what was left of the regiments passed between Flavigny and Vionville and was rallied in the bottom to the southwest of the latter place. Smaller detachments and individual dispersed men reached our infantry, which fought east of the Tronville copses, and rejoined their regiments by way of Mars-la-Tour.

Three platoons were formed of the remnants of the *cuirassiers*. Upon arrival of the 3rd squadron, which had been sent against the Tronville copses, and of the first platoon of the 1st squadron, which had been detached on relay service, the regiment was formed in 2 squadrons of 4 platoons of 11 files, altogether 220 men of all ranks.

Deducting the scattered men which rejoined during the next few days, the losses of the regiment were as follows: dead, 1 officer, 43 men, 33 horses; wounded, 6 officers, 72 men, 25 horses; missing. 83 men, 203 horses; total, 7 officers, 198 men, 261 horses.

Second-Lieutenants von Ploetz and Count Sierstorpf died of their wounds; Captain Meyer was among the killed.

Six officers and 80 men of the 16th Ulans assembled at first near Flavigny; 2 officers and 15 men rejoined by way of Mars-la-Tour. Upon the arrival of the 1st squadron, which had been sent against the Tronville copses, and of a few other detachments, the regiment had in ranks in the evening 12 officers and 210 men, many of whom were

---

than 400 to 500 horses, dependent upon whether they consisted of four or five squadrons; that the dragoon regiments of Murat's Brigade of De Forton's Division had suffered not inconsiderable losses that morning near Vionville, and had therefore not more than 500 horses in ranks; that one squadron of the 4th Regiment of Chasseurs à Cheval of De Valabrègue's (1st) Brigade had been detached as escort to Marshal Bazaine, and that this regiment had no more than 400 horses in its four squadrons—still those eight regiments numbered: —
1st and 9th Dragoons, each 4 squadrons, @ 300. . . 600 horses.—7th and 10th Cuirassiers, each 4 squadrons, 400. . 800 horses.—4th Chasseurs à Cheval, 4 squadrons. 400 horses.—5th Chasseurs à Cheval, 5 squadrons 500 horses.—7th and 12th Dragoons, each 4 squadrons, @ 400 . . 800 horses.—Total, 3,100 horses. As against these the Prussian horsemen rode in 23 platoons, 11 of the 7th Cuirassiers, and 12 of the 16th Ulans.
According to the last preceding return of the 5th Cavalry Division, dated August 11th, the regiments of the same numbered on an average 560 horses, which gives 35 horses per platoon (16 platoons in a regiment), and for these 23 platoons 805 horses. Considering the losses suffered by these squadrons before coming in collision with the enemy's cavalry, which would leave little over 600 horses, an estimate of five-fold superiority on the part of the French cavalry is hardly placed too high.

slightly wounded.

Deducting the men who rejoined later, the losses of the regiment are as follows: dead, 2 officers, 28 men, 172 horses; wounded, 5 officers, 101 men, 28 horses; missing, 2 officers, 54 men; total, 9 officers, 183 men, 200 horses.

Second-Lieutenants von Roman and von Gellhorn were killed.

The regimental commander, Von der Dollen, was missing, and also Second-Lieutenant Vogt; they were lying wounded and helpless under their dead horses and fell in the enemy's hands.

The French account, in its more poetic style, calls this ride of the Prussian horsemen a "Death ride" (*chevauchade de mort*); the Prussian account, with its characteristic language, which confines itself strictly to facts, says:

But we are disencumbered—from this direction no more attacks are made today.

This was the result of the "Death ride" for our lines; those of the enemy had been broken through (*traversé*); his batteries, in spite of their well-aimed fire, had been cut down (*sabré*); his own horsemen, five-fold superior to the Prussians, fresh, and who could only have had to do with the rinsings of this wave of horsemen, had to be re-formed (*reformé*) and withdrawn to the bottom of Gravelotte, a half a mile from the field of battle.

The 7th Cuirassiers and the 16th Ulans may well be proud of this "Death ride," the whole Prussian cavalry may be proud of it, for all its regiments would have done the same; of this the day of Vionville and Mars-la-Tour bears ample testimony.

In further execution of the above (mentioned earlier) order of Lieutenant-General von Alvensleben, the 11th Brigade had, simultaneously with the advance of the 12th Brigade toward Vionville, moved by the west of the Tronville copses toward Bruville to the point where the 13th Dragoons were already in observation to meet any danger to the left flank of the fighting troops. Here the brigade took position in closed line of squadrons in platoon columns to the right rear of the 13th Dragoons, the 19th Regiment forward on the *plateau* overlooking the valley extending from St. Marcel to Bruville, on their right rear the 13th Ulans, on their left rear the 4th Cuirassiers.

Soon after the brigade had taken position in this manner, it was joined by the 1st Horse Battery of the Guard, Captain von der Planitz, which enabled the brigade to remain as long as it did in its exposed position, which would have been impossible without artillery. The battery at once, directed its fire against the hostile batteries posted south of St. Marcel, drawing their fire on itself and diverting it from the infantry, which was advancing south of the Tronville copses, and frustrated the attack of a hostile battalion which threatened the battery's right flank from a wood south of St. Marcel. The 19th Dragoons, specially charged with the escort of this battery, repeatedly repulsed, by short charges, strong hostile skirmish lines which attempted to advance from St. Marcel.

Meanwhile also the closed masses of the enemy's infantry approached nearer and nearer from Bruville, and more particularly from St. Marcel, covered by bushes, hedges, and a field covered with rows of sheaves; the fire of the skirmishers began to reach the regiments of the 11th Brigade; officers, men, and horses were wounded and killed. Finally, when the supports of the enemy's line began to fire volleys into the brigade and a *mitrailleuse* battery also opened, it withdrew slowly in the direction of Tronville. The 13th Dragoons, though belonging to the 12th Brigade, joined in the movement of the 11th Brigade. The battery of Captain von der Planitz retreated in the direction of Mars-la-Tour, came in action again for a short time north of this place, and then joined the 1st Dragoons of the Guard, with whom it had originally arrived on the battlefield.[50]

The arrival of the 20th Infantry Division at Tronville, and its advance against the great *chaussée* and the copses to the north of the same, made the further presence of the 11th Cavalry Brigade at this point needless. In order not to expose it to further useless losses, the brigade was withdrawn to the southwest of Tronville and took position, 13th Ulans, 13th and 19th Dragoons, in the angle between the highroads Buxières—Mars-la-Tour and Puxieux—Tronville, and to the north of the latter. The 4th Cuirassiers were posted at the southeast corner of Tronville, near the Gorze road, in support of the 20th Infantry Division and as right flank guard of the batteries of the 10th Corps, which were in action north of the village.

The brigade here also came in touch with the 10th Hussars, belonging to the 13th Brigade, who had withdrawn to the deep ground north of Puxieux. when their exposed position between the great *chaussée* and the southernmost part of the Tronville copses was rendered untenable by the progress which the infantry fight made inside the wood.

---

50. Compare footnote 51.

The batteries of the 10th Corps mentioned, having been reinforced by two additional batteries, advanced for the present to, and subsequently beyond, the great *chaussée* between Mars-la-Tour and the Tronville copses.

The commanding general of the 10th Corps, General of Infantry von Voigts-Rhetz, who had been on the field for some time, directed that two squadrons of the 4th Cuirassiers cover these batteries on the left, toward Mars-la-Tour. The 4th and 5th squadrons were detailed for this duty; they trotted forward in the direction of Mars-la-Tour about 4 p. m., under command of Major von Kuylenstierna, and took position at the northwest corner of the southern one of the copses.

Soon afterward Von Wedell's (38th) Brigade of Lieutenant-General von Schwarzkoppen's (19th) Infantry Division reached Mars-la-Tour and advanced in deployed line of battle against the hostile divisions of Grenier and Cissey of the 4th Corps (De Ladmirault's), which had moved forward to the height south of the farmstead of Gréyère. The heroic attack failed on account of the enemy's enormous superiority of numbers and position. The *débris* poured back toward Mars-la-Tour and across the *chaussée*, briskly pursued by the enemy.

Again it fell to the lot of the cavalry to restore the fight by throwing itself into the dangerous gap.

The Dragoon Brigade of the Guard[51] had been placed under the orders of the 10th Corps on the 15th of August, and had started with it from Thiaucourt early on the 16th in the direction of Fresnes en Woévre.

The 2nd squadron of the 2nd Dragoons of the Guard did not march with it, but had, as above mentioned, marched with two horse batteries of the 10th Corps, under the direction of Lieutenant-Colonel von Caprivi, to join the 5th Cavalry Division, and, in conjunction with the 13th Brigade, found repeated opportunity to take a distinguished part in the mounted conflicts near Vionville and Flavigny. The remaining three squadrons were attached to the 19th Infantry Division (Von Schwarzkoppen's), whose divisional cavalry regiment (the 9th Dragoons) was already in action on the battlefield in conjunction with the detachment of Colonel von Lynker at the point where the latter attacked in conjunction with the 6th Cavalry Division, (compare with earlier mention).

These three squadrons constituted the advance guard, the point being formed by the 3rd squadron (Captain John's), from which a

---

51. 1st and 2nd Dragoons of the Guard, 1st Horse Battery of the Guard.

platoon was detached to the right to establish communication with Colonel Lehmann's detachment. The rest of the squadron General of Infantry von Voigts-Rhetz took with him as escort, when he left the line of march of the division which he had accompanied, in order to ride toward the sound of the guns coming from Metz and to convince himself by personal inspection of its import. The squadron remained with him during the subsequent course of the battle, came under effective hostile fire, and suffered some losses, particularly when temporarily escorting a battery of the 10th Corps which was advancing without special escort; but it had no opportunity to take an active part. Two of its officers, the Second Lieutenants von Tümpling and Count zu Stolberg, were dispatched to guide the 1st Dragoons of the Guard with the battery of Von der Planitz, and the 19th Infantry Division, respectively, to the battlefield.

The 5th squadron (Captain von Trotha's) took the lead in place of the 3rd. Upon arrival at Marchéville en Woëvre, it posted outposts to cover the troops of the division which were going into bivouac. The latter, however,, was soon abandoned, and the march resumed in an easterly direction toward Mars-la-Tour.

The 1st Dragoons of the Guard with the battery of Captain von der Planitz had preceded the division in the direction of St. Hilaire, and were resting there when the latter arrived. The sound of guns resounding from the direction of Metz had been heard here for some time, but it did not seem advisable to march toward it, as the head of the 19th Infantry Division would have been uncovered. When the latter reached St. Hilaire, permission to march in the direction of Metz was requested and granted.

While the 19th Infantry Division, with whom the 4th and 5th squadrons of the 2nd Dragoons of the Guard had remained, was posting outposts near Marchéville,[52] the 1st Dragoons of the Guard and the battery of Von der Planitz trotted briskly toward the sound of the guns.

They were soon followed by the 19th Infantry Division, which had received orders from its commanding general to hasten to the battlefield. To re-establish communication with the 1st Dragoons of the Guard, the 4th squadron of the 2nd Dragoons of the Guard, under Captain von Hindenburg, was at once sent after them; it was accompanied by the regimental commander, Colonel von Finkentein. The 5th squadron remained with the 19th Infantry Division, and marched

52. Near St. Hilaire on the Verdun Road.

at the head of the column.

When about half a mile west of Mars-la-Tour, this squadron was sent off to the north to reconnoitre toward Jarny. At Ville sur Yron it observed hostile cavalry, and remained there for further observation.

As the 1st Dragoons of the Guard and the battery of Von der Planitz on their march toward the sound of the guns approached Mars-la-Tour, dense clouds of dust became visible north of the woods in the direction of Jarny.[53] They could not but be caused by considerable bodies of troops, which were probably marching away on the *chaussée* Metz—Etain.

It was the duty of the cavalry to investigate; should appearances turn out true, ,the cavalry might contribute materially toward checking the enemy's retreat. The dragoon regiment and the battery therefore turned off to the left from a point close to the west of Mars-la-Tour. The 4th squadron of the 2nd Dragoons of the Guard, just arrived from the 19th Infantry Division, took the lead as advance guard, followed by the 1st Dragoons of the Guard in closed line of squadrons in platoon columns, and by the battery of Captain von der Planitz, and thus they moved along the *chaussée* to Jarny.

On reaching Ville sur Yron, hostile cavalry was perceived in the woods north of that place. This cavalry threw out scouts, as did the Prussians, since reconnaissance was required here, and the enemy's closed bodies did not leave the wood and failed to offer an objective for a charge.

Captain von der Planitz, who did not find here an opportunity for the action of his battery and was attracted by the artillery conflict raging in the direction of St. Marcel, requested and received permission to take part there. The very effective part taken by this battery has been detailed above, (compare earlier mention). Meanwhile the hostile artillery continued to gain ground between Bruville and St. Marcel, and its shells began to reach the dragoons of the Prussian Guard near Ville sur Yron.

The French account here states:

On reaching the farmstead of Gréyère, General de Ladmirault examines the battlefield. . . . . . he crosses the ravine, taking with him a 12-pounder battery, which drove back two Prussian dragoon regiments that were approaching.

The account is somewhat in error, in that it was not two regiments

---

53. On the road loading north from Mars-la-Tour.

that approached, but five squadrons belonging to two different regiments.

They withdrew slowly toward Mars-la-Tour, and took position southwest of the village. The battery of Captain von der Planitz, which had been forced to retreat, (as mentioned earlier), here joined them, and a little later the heads of the 19th Infantry Division also arrived.

The commander of the latter, Lieutenant-General von Schwarzkoppen, on going to the front to reconnoitre, perceived the closed masses of the 20th Infantry Division in the direction of Tronville; according to the information received, he had to believe his left flank covered toward Ville sur Yron by cavalry (5th Cavalry Division). He therefore decided to launch his attack between the two, passing by the east of Mars-la-Tour.

The dragoons of the Guard were therefore directed to advance by the west of Mars-la-Tour, to accompany the attack of the 38th Brigade on the left, and to close the gap between the latter and the cavalry supposed to be at Ville sur Yron.

In execution of these various arrangements the 38th Infantry Brigade began its bold attack soon after 4 p. m.

At the same time the brigade commander, Major-General Count von Brandenburg, who was with the 1st Dragoons of the Guard, ordered the battery of Captain von der Planitz forward to prepare the advance of the regiment and to come into action north of Mars-la-Tour against the hostile cavalry, which had advanced in closed masses to the farmstead of Gréyère. The regimental commander, Colonel Count von Finkenstein, joined the 4th squadron of the 2nd Dragoons of the Guard, which escorted the battery.

The battery came into action north of Mars-la-Tour on the *chaussée* to Jarny, near height 230, and a few shots sufficed to cause the enemy's cavalry to withdraw behind the height on which the farmstead is situated. In order to renew its fire against this cavalry, the battery, accompanied by the squadron, galloped forward about 600 paces on the *chaussée*, wheeled to the right so as to front parallel to the *chaussée*, and opened fire against the French cavalry, which had again come in view, and against other large bodies of the enemy's right wing.

The 1st Dragoons of the Guard, however, did not accompany that movement, having been recalled from this direction after taking it. The regiment was ordered to take a position covering the left flank of the artillery of the 10th Corps, which had advanced beyond the great *chaussée*, and, while carrying out the order, met, to the southwest of Mars-la-Tour, the two squadrons of the 4th Cuirassiers which had been sent there ere this, (compare earlier mention).

The attack of the 38th Infantry Brigade was dashed to pieces. The 1st Dragoons of the Guard, posted southeast of Mars-la-Tour, received orders from General of Infantry von Voigts-Rhetz to protect the remnants, and to stem the enemy's pursuit, no matter at what cost.

It was about 5 p. m. when this order was received. The regiment was in line of squadrons in platoon columns with deploying intervals, the 1st squadron on the right, each squadron right in front. The regimental adjutant, Second Lieutenant von Dachroeden, was sent forward to reconnoitre the ground and the enemy's position and to furnish the regimental commander, Colonel von Auerswald, the requisite information as to the direction to be taken under the circumstances. He returned with the report that dense bodies of hostile infantry were briskly pursuing the 38th Infantry Brigade and advancing against the heights east of Mars-la-Tour, and that the terrain on the east of the village was cut up with hedges and ditches and extremely unfavourable to the movements of cavalry.

In spite of these not very promising circumstances, Colonel von Auerswald did not hesitate a moment to carry out his order. The regiment moved forward to the northeast in platoon column, past Mars-la-Tour, the 5th squadron leading, next the 3rd, and then the 1st squadron; the 4th remained back as reserve. In order to overcome the difficulties of the terrain, column of threes had to be formed, and then again column of platoons under the effective fire of hostile batteries in action north of the Ulzon Brook,[54] so that the regiment became somewhat strung out, despite the best efforts of the squadrons to keep closed up.

When the first platoon of the 5th squadron got clear of the difficult ground, and reached the edge of the heights to the north of the *chaussée* to Vionville. it was given such a direction by Colonel von Auerswald as would, when wheeling into line for the charge as contemplated, bring it opposite the right of the victoriously advancing infantry masses of the enemy.

The rear platoons had to gallop throughout in order not to lose distance.

The 13th Regiment of the Line, of the French Brigade of Bellecourt of the 2nd (Grenier's) Division of the 4th Army Corps, was

---

54. Evidently the small brook north of the village. The name is not on the official maps.—A. L. W.

in immediate pursuit of the 38th Prussian Infantry Brigade and had crossed the ravine (deep, with steep sides) of the Ulzon Brook and continued to advance southward on the *plateau*, while the 43rd Regiment of the Line remained north of this ravine in second line, and parts of the 5th Chasseur battalion was pushing forward toward Mars-la-Tour in the bushy valley. This infantry, particularly the skirmishers of the 13th Regiment of the Line, were directing a severe fire on the 1st Dragoons of the Guard during the movement just described. The losses increased every minute.

Under these circumstances, Colonel von Auerswald deemed it necessary to reach the enemy as quickly as possible, and ordered the platoons to wheel right into line before the 1st squadron had completely cleared the difficult ground. As soon as sufficient ground had been gained, the chief of this squadron, Count Wesdehlen, ordered the platoons to wheel right into line, and followed the preceding squadrons, which had formed line ere this, in such a manner that during the ensuing advance the right flank of his squadron skirted the road to St. Marcel. The regiment was thus in proper order of battle, the 1st squadron on the right, but the squadrons were inverted, the 1st platoon being on the left.

Soon after the 3rd and 5th squadrons had formed line, the signal "Gallop!" was given, followed immediately by "March! March!" The 1st squadron followed a moment later, upon command or signal by its chief.

The brigade commander (who was present) and his staff joined the charge on the right of the regiment.

As the regiment rushed upon them, the hostile skirmishers fell back on their supports, formed groups, and opened a destructive fire on the dragoons, while a *mitrailleuse* battery north of the Ulzon Brook fired volley after volley into their left flank. Nevertheless, though with terribly thinned ranks, the brave regiment broke into the hostile infantry and whirled it, to use the language of the French account around its eagles. Some of the horsemen passed between the groups and succumbed to the bullets of the second French line. But the enemy's advance was checked; the Prussian infantry was disengaged, and the task of the regiment gloriously accomplished.

Its remnants, almost without leaders, as eleven officers were *hors de combat*, fell back on Mars-la-Tour, suffering additional heavy losses in doing so. On the spot from which this magnificent charge had started, Captain Prince von Hohenzollern rallied the remnants of the three squadrons, which had charged, around his own (4th) squadron, which had remained in reserve. The regimental commander, Colonel von Auerswald, himself fatally wounded, addressed words of thanks and appreciation to his brave regiment, called for a rousing cheer for the King, and then sank from his horse, never to mount again.

Almost a third of the brave horsemen were lying on the field: dead, 5 officers, 1 ensign, 42 men, 204 horses; wounded, 6 officers, 2 ensigns, 76 men, 42 horses; missing, 5 men; total, 11 officers, 3 ensigns, 123 men, 246 horses.

The killed were Major von Kleist, the Captains and Squadron Commanders Count Westarp, Henry XVII. Prince of Reuss, Count Wesdehlen, the Second Lieutenant von Treskow, and Ensign von Treskow. Colonel von Auerswald, First Lieutenant Count Schwerin, and Second Lieutenant Count Solms-Sonnenwalde (whose appointment reached him just before his death) succumbed to their wounds, while the Second Lieutenants von Rohr 3rd, von Kroecher, Count Strachwitz, and Count Stolberg-Rosla, and Ensign Count Bismarck I.[55] (who was doing officer's duty) recovered.

One squadron was formed of the remnants of the three which had charged; it withdrew to Xonville in company with the 4th squadron, both bivouacking there in the evening.

Captain Prince von Hohenzollern assumed command of the regiment.

The 4th and 5th squadrons of the 4th Cuirassiers endeavoured to join the charge of the 1st Dragoons of the Guard on the right; but, receiving severe infantry and *mitrailleuse* fire from front and flank, their advance, however brave,, could have no important result. They withdrew, leaving three officers wounded, and some thirty men and horses dead and wounded, on the field, and re-formed near Tronville, where they met the remaining two squadrons of the regiment late in the evening.

According to the accounts of the 5th Cavalry Division, it was not until this time that Major-General von Barby received orders to advance, with the regiments he then had with him, by the west of Mars-la-Tour, to prevent the enemy's further advance by pressure upon his right.

The 13th Dragoons (posted on the left) leading, in their rear the 13th Ulans and 19th Dragoons, then the 1st and 3rd squadrons of

---

55. Son of the German Chancellor. Another son rode in the ranks as a private.—A. L. W.

the 4th Cuirassiers, the 10th Hussars and 16th Dragoons[56] all trotted off in a north-westerly direction, skirted Mars-la-Tour on the south, and, when north of the *chaussée* to Verdun, advanced over the western slopes of the height, the 13th Dragoons skirting the Mars-la-Tour—Jarny *chaussée*.

In first line are: on the right the 19th Dragoons, then the two squadrons of the 4th Cuirassiers, on the left the 13th Ulans; in second line: on the right the 10th Hussars, numbering but three squadrons, on the left the 16th Dragoons. The formation was in part open, in part closed line of squadrons in platoon columns.

While passing by Mars-la-Tour the 3rd squadron of the 13th Ulans (Captain Schlick's) was detached to the 19th Infantry Division, which was without cavalry and needed it urgently, to assemble with its assistance the dispersed remnants of the 38th Brigade.

The 13th Dragoons came in touch with the enemy before long. For a proper understanding of this and subsequent events, some knowledge of what meanwhile happened on the enemy's side is requisite.

It has been stated above, (compare earlier mention), that General de Ladmirault hurried forward in advance of his (4th) corps, which had turned off to the left from the Gravelotte—Doncourt *chaussée* and was marching on Bruville, and placed a 12-pounder battery in action at the Gréyère farm against the 1st Dragoons of the Guard. The appearance of hostile troops on his right made him uneasy for his battery, and he ordered the 5th Battalion of Foot Chasseurs of the 1st (Bellecourt's) Brigade of the 2nd (Grenier's) Division into the valley intervening between the heights of Gréyère and Ville sur Yron, and posted the 98th Regiment of the Line of the 2nd (Pradier's) Brigade of the same division in the farmstead. As this failed to satisfy him, he decided to oppose all his available cavalry to the opponent, who threatened his flank.

The French account states:

About 500 meters from the farmstead of Gréyère, in rear of our right flank, was the 2nd Regiment of Chasseurs d'Afrique under the command of General du Barail. They were subsequently joined by Legrand's Division.[57] with the exception of the 11th

---

56. Divisional cavalry regiment of the 20th Infantry Division.

57. Cavalry division of the 4th Corps: General Legrand, Chief of Staff, Colonel Campenon.—1st brigade: General de Montaigu, 2nd Hussars, 7th Hussars.—2nd brigade: General de Gondrecourt, 3rd Dragoons, 11th Dragoons.—Total, 1,800 horses.

Dragoons, which were in reserve in rear of the infantry. General de France, with the dragoons and lancers of the Guard, was also on the height. Lastly, De Clérembault's Division[58] of the 3rd Army Corps was near Bruville. The *chasseur* regiments of this division had been weakened by detachments furnished to the Infantry Divisions. De Juniac's Brigade was at the time with Marshal Leboeuf, commander of the 3rd Army Corps.[59]

Toward 4:30 p. m. a battery separated itself from the hostile cavalry to take us in right flank, and took position on the road about abreast of the farmstead of Gréyère.[60] To silence its fire, General de Ladmirault directed the Generals du Barail, Legrand, and De France to disencumber his right flank. General du Barail crossed the valley with the 2nd Chasseurs d'Afrique, wheeled to the left, and, charging as foragers (*en fourageurs*), threw himself on the guns, which had barely time to fire; the *chasseurs* cut down those artillerists who had no time to escape, but, meeting superior forces,[61] they turned off to the right, assembled in the angle between the road and the wood.[62] and held the enemy

---

58. Cavalry division of the 3rd Corps: General de Clérembault, Chief of Staff, Colonel Jouffroy d'Abbaus.—1st brigade: General de Bruchard, 2nd Chasseurs, 3rd Chasseurs, 10th Chasseurs.—2nd brigade: General de Maubranches, 2nd Dragoons, 4th Dragoons.—3rd brigade: General de Juniac, 5th Dragoons, 8th Dragoons.— Total, 3,100 horses.

59. On the French side the following cavalry, which was entirely fresh and had not yet been under fire, was therefore assembled near the farmstead of Gréyère and available at any moment:—2nd Chasseurs d'Afrique, 5 squadrons 500 horses.—2nd and 7th Hussars, 5 squadrons each, @ 500 1,000 horses.—3rd Dragoons, 4 squadrons 400 horses.—Dragoons and Lancers of the Guard, each 5 squadrons, @ 500 1,000 horses.—Total in first line 2,900 horses.—2nd, 3rd, and 10th Chasseurs à Cheval, each 4 squadrons, detachments having been furnished to the infantry, @ 400 1,200 horses.—2nd and 4th Dragoons, each 4 squadrons, @ 400. . . 800 horses.— Total in second line 2,000 horses.—Grand total. . . 4,900 horses.—As against this cavalry there were brought forward by Major-General von Barby, or were near Ville sur Yron, the following regiments, all of which had been under fire and in the saddle since daybreak, the strength being based on the average strength given in the return for August 11th:—19th Dragoons 560 horses.—13th Ulans (3 squadrons) 420 horses.—4th Cuirassiers (2 squadrons) 280 horses.—13th Dragoons 560 horses.—10th Hussars (3 squadrons) 420 horses.—16th Dragoons 560 horses.—2nd Dragoons of the Guard (2 squadrons) 280 horses.—Total, 3,080 horses.—*Not counting the losses already suffered on this day.*

60. Battery Planitz.

61. 13th Dragoons; compare footnote 58.

62. Meaning the wood of Gréyère north of Ville sur Yron.

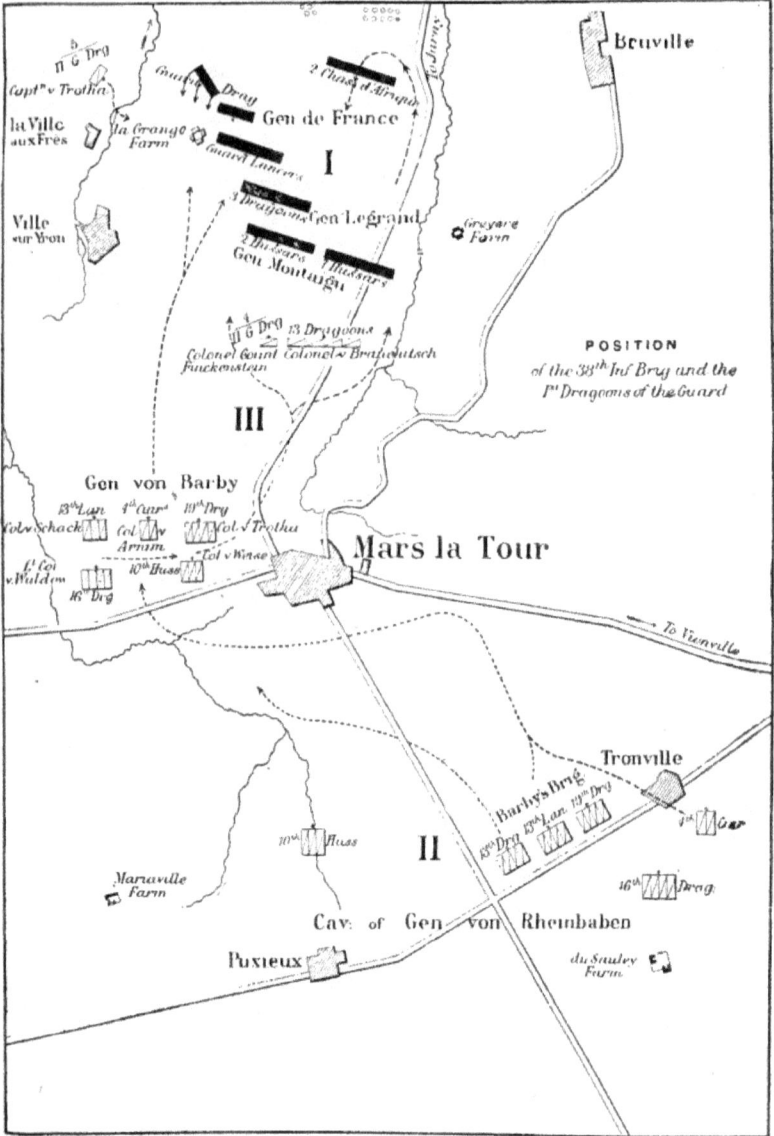

VON BARBY'S CHARGE

in check by a brisk fire. *After this splendid feat, the battery did not again make its appearance.*

Let us see what the Prussian accounts have to say of this splendid feat, the non-reappearance of the battery.

We left the battery of Captain von der Planitz at the moment when it took up its second position against the enemy's masses of cavalry near the farmstead of Gréyère. Soon afterward a hostile company deployed as skirmishers near the farmstead and directed a very accurate fire against the battery[63] while almost at the same time the 2nd Chasseurs d'Afrique charged it on the left.

The 4th squadron of the 2nd Dragoons of the Guard advanced to meet them and broke the force of the charge, so that the battery gained time to withdraw and take up a position close to Mars-la-Tour on the north of the village for the protection of the regiments which now took part in the action, under Major-General von Barby's leadership.

The success of the *chasseurs d'Afrique* was not such as it appeared to the latter, for, according to the official returns, the battery lost: dead, 3 horses; wounded, 3 men, 4 horses; total, 3 men, 7 horses. These losses, the battery commander expressly states, "were caused exclusively by the infantry skirmishers firing on the battery."

On perceiving the great superiority of the attacking enemy over his own single squadron, and probably also the approach of the remaining hostile regiments, which, as we shall see below, had put themselves in motion soon after the *chasseurs d'Afrique*, Colonel Count von Finkenstein hastened to the rear in the direction of Mars-la-Tour, where he had noticed the 13th Dragoons, which, at the head of the regiments of Major-General von Barby, came in view this moment.

On his request, the regiment attacked at once, released the 4th squadron of the 2nd Dragoons of the Guard, which had been borne along by the enemy's superior numbers, and drove back the French *chasseurs*, now themselves defenceless, owing to the winded state of the horses and the disorder resulting from the attack, without difficulty, and with such vigour that, according to French accounts, they retreated as far as the wood of Gréyère and contented themselves with mere fire-action.

The brave 2nd Dragoons had paid dearly for their heroic devotion to the battery entrusted to their care. The leader of the 4th squadron

---

63. Probably a company of the 5th Battalion of Foot Chasseurs, which had been ordered into the valley by General de Ladmirault.

(Captain von Hindenburg) and several dragoons were killed, and three officers and many men and horses were wounded.

Those hostile squadrons whose approach Colonel Count von Finkenstein had observed were now about to come into action.

While the 2nd Chasseurs d'Afrique were making their attack on the battery of Captain von der Planitz, the French division of Legrand, which we left in position north of the farmstead of Gréyère, wheeled by platoons to the right, crossed the ravine and road, and, when south of the wood of Gréyère, wheeled by platoons to the left, the 3rd Dragoons in second line and overlapping the right of De Montaigu's Hussar Brigade. At the same time De France's Brigade (lancers and dragoons of the Guard) marched by the right flank, crossed the ravine to the right of Legrand's Division, the lancers leading, and, after passing along the rear of Legrand, came into line on his right rear; the lancer regiment in first line, the dragoons in second line, each overlapping the right of the regiment in its front. [64]

While engaged in the pursuit of the *chasseurs d'Afrique*, the 13th Prussian Dragoons perceived the just described deployment of the hostile cavalry. Colonel von Brauchitsch had the rally sounded at once and assembled the regiment about Ville sur Yron.

Meanwhile General Legrand had received repeated orders from his commanding general to charge without delay. With reference to the quick rally of the Prussian dragoons, General du Barail said: "It is too late; the opportunity is past." A colonel of hussars requested permission to shake the enemy first by carbine fire, and thus prepare the charge in view of the considerable distance of 2,000 paces measured on the air-line. General Legrand, however, full of ardour, exclaimed: "*Non; au sabre!*" and ordered General de Montaigu to lead his brigade against the enemy. It advanced at a gallop, a portion still in column with half distances, not well closed, but with spirit and dash.

"The German dragoons," says Lieutenant-Colonel Bonie,[65] "awaited the charge on the spot,[66] and outlined against the sky like giants (*comme des colosses*). When our hussars had approached

---

64. The French cavalry was thus formed in four lines: in first line, De Montaigu's Hussar Brigade; in second line and overlapping the former's right, the 3rd Dragoons; in third line,, the lancers of the Guard, overlapping the right of the dragoons; in fourth line, the dragoons of the Guard, overlapping the right of the lancers.
65. 13th Dragoons and 4th squadron of the 2nd Dragoons of the Guard.
66. In addition to the considerable distance of 2,000 paces, the French hussars had the disadvantage of charging up hill.

within a few paces, the Prussian dragoons gave a terrible cheer, opened fire from their short carbines, which were attached to the saddle,[67] quickly took their sabres in hand, and descended in formidable array."

The commander of the 13th Dragoons soon noticed that the hostile hussars, while advancing, endeavoured to gain the right flank of his regiment. To frustrate the attempt, he wheeled by platoons to the right, trotted for some distance to the right, wheeled into line and threw himself at a gallop upon the enemy, who was quite close by that time. The 4th squadron of the 2nd Dragoons of the Guard, led by Col. Count von Finkenstein, charged on the left of the 13th Dragoons.

The French account continues:

The collision was terrible; the mass of our small horses, winded by the long charge, breaks against this wall, which the enemy, much larger of stature, opposes. The 7th Hussars turn off partly into a gap, partly against another hostile regiment approaching rapidly in close column.

This hostile regiment consisted of the three squadrons of the 10th Hussars. Leaving the regiments assembled at Mars-la-Tour, the 10th Hussars arrived in rear of the 13th Dragoons in line of squadrons in platoon columns with deploying intervals at the moment when this regiment wheeled by platoons to the right. That movement unmasked the 3rd and (afterward) the 4th squadron of the Hussars (Captain von Kotze and First Lieutenant von Lübbe),[68] which at once formed line, and, wheeling half right, attacked the French hussars, which had passed partly through the gaps of the 13th Dragoons, partly around the left flank of the 4th squadron of the 2nd Dragoons of the Guard, and thus took them in right flank.

This action of the hussar squadrons was all the more timely, as the ranks of the 13th Dragoons had become somewhat loosened by the bold movement carried out at a distance of a few hundred paces from the enemy, who was charging full tilt.

The 2nd squadron, under First Lieutenant von Redern, was dispatched to the right flank of the dragoons by Colonel von Weise, the regimental commander. Its 4th platoon, led in person by the former squadron chief, Captain von Heister, now on duty as general staff of-

---

67. Probably an error, already cleared up in *Reflections on the Formation, Employment, and Action of Cavalry, etc.*, 1st pamphlet of the *Militaer Wochenblatt* for 1872.
68. Led the squadron in place of Captain von Kaisenberg, who was wounded.

ficer of the 5th Cavalry Division, joined the right of the dragoons to meet any outflanking movement on that side. The remaining three platoons, while still in the act of forming line by the side of the fourth, encountered hostile hussars, which here also had penetrated through the gaps or had passed by the right of the dragoons, threw them back, and thus took the enemy in left flank.

The attack of the French hussars was repulsed by the 13th Dragoons and 2nd Dragoons of the Guard, and, taken in both flanks by the 10th Hussars, they fled after a short *mêlée* toward the wood, briskly pursued, particularly by the Prussian hussars, as far as the deep ravine which the French regiments had crossed shortly before; there the *chasseurs d'Afrique*, rallied by this time, received the Prussian hussars with a severe fire.

General de Montaigu came to the ground severely wounded, and Lieutenant von Wedell, of the 10th Hussars, received his sword, which he had wielded so bravely. Colonel Count von Finkenstein received several wounds and was killed, as was Major von Hertell, of the 10th Hussars.

On seeing the ill success of his hussars, General Legrand placed himself at the head of the 3rd Dragoons and threw himself on the Prussian dragoons and hussars; the left wing of the regiment was carried away in part by the retreating French, in part by the 10th Prussian Hussars. Pierced by a sword, the general died the beautiful death of a soldier at the head of his troops.

The 19th (Oldenburg) Dragoons, mentioned above as on the right of the regiments led forward by Major-General von Barby, also advanced,—leading perhaps slightly the 10th Hussars,—formed line abreast of Ville sur Yron, and, so far, had followed the charge of the 13th Dragoons and 10th Hussars at a trot. It now prepared to charge the French lancers of the Guard, which had wheeled into line and were advancing slowly.

They (the Oldenburg Dragoons) were taken in right flank by the two right squadrons of the 3rd French Dragoons under General Legrand, which had preserved their formation. First Lieutenant Haake, leader of the 1st squadron, noticed it in time, wheeled half right, and, throwing himself at a gallop on the hostile dragoons, broke through them.

The remaining three squadrons of the 19th Dragoons, admirably closed up, continued their charge against the lancers. They had been led forward in great haste by General de France; their left wing became entangled with General Legrand's dragoons and their centre was pierced by the Prussian 19th Dragoons. Almost at the same time the three squadrons of the Prussian 13th Ulans had come up. Forming line shortly after the 19th Dragoons, and probably on the same spot, and ordered to gain the enemy's right flank, they came on at the long gallop against the right wing of the French lancers. Wheeling slightly half right, Captain von Trzebinski threw himself on them with the 1st squadron.

The remaining two squadrons (2nd and 4th, Captains von Durant and von Rosenberg) continued straight to the front and struck the French dragoons of the Guard, who came toward them at a trot and not with any too great *élan*. The 2nd squadron of the 13th Ulans went straight against them; the 4th took them in right flank, wherein they were assisted by the 5th squadron of the 2nd Dragoons of the Guard (Captain von Trotha),[69] which galloped forward in platoon column on the left of the 13th Ulans, took a hedge 3½ feet high, wheeled into line to the right, and, passing around the farmstead of La Grange, attacked the French dragoons in rear.

The two squadrons of the 4th Cuirassiers, originally between the 19th Dragoons and 13th Ulans, had been crowded out of the line, as the ground toward the farmstead of La Orange narrowed considerably, and were unable to deploy. One in rear of the other, each in line, they threw themselves in the *mêlée* at the point where the 1st squadron of the 13th Ulans was engaged with the French dragoons and lancers of the Guard.

About the same time the French *Chasseurs d'Afrique,* which had been rallied, reappeared on the field.

The second line on the Prussian side had been formed in the first place, as we know, by the 10th Hussars (on the right) and 16th Dragoons (on the left). The hussars we have seen engaged in the general conflict; they were soon followed by the dragoons, who state that they were chiefly engaged with lancers and 7th Hussars of the enemy. It is probable, therefore, that they struck that point of the enemy's line where Legrand's Division and De France's Brigade had become intermixed. They too broke through the enemy, and their main body

---

69. This squadron had been detached on reconnaissance to the left of the line of march on the 19th Infantry Division, and we know that until now it had remained near Ville sur Yron, keeping a sharp eye on the enemy. As General von Barby's regiments approached, it joined the left of the 13th Ulans and advanced with them on their left front.

joined the hussars in the pursuit of the hostile horsemen as far as the ravine opposite the farmstead of Gréyère.

It was no longer a mere attack, a mere conflict; it was a dizzy, whirling throng of battle, a furious tornado, in which 6,000 horsemen of all colours and of all arms slaughtered each other, some with the point, others with the full weight of the sword.

Thus Lieutenant-Colonel Bonie paints with poetical language this wild, surging conflict on the bloody field strewn with corpses and torn by the horses' hoofs.

On account of their light blue uniforms, the French lancers were mistaken by their own countrymen for Prussian dragoons, and cut down without mercy. On the other hand, the Prussian 19th Dragoons suffered no small losses from the thrusts of their lances.

The French dragoons of the Guard are of the opinion that they annihilated the Prussian 13th Ulans (*les abîment*); the latter state the following about their collision with the dragoons of the Empress:

What enormous difference! Our men, so frequently avoided in the past by hostile cavalry, and impatient of restraint, gave a ringing cheer when yet at a distance, barely waiting for the squadron leaders command, 'March! March!' The French dragoons made the impression as though they possessed the determination not to turn about, but could not muster the requisite energy to advance.[70]

But who would undertake to decide that today? It is certain, however, that the Prussian *ulan* regiment brought back from the fight hostile officers and many other prisoners, as well as captured horses, while all French reports that have become public so far fail to mention proof of similar good results.

"Seeing the terrible *mêlée*," continues the French account,[71] "General de France has the recall sounded and our men return in disorder (*désordre*) to re-form at about the point whence the

---

70. The 13th Ulans claim to have been engaged with hostile *chasseurs*, in addition to the dragoons of the Guard, and to have seen some squadrons of hostile *cuirassiers* by the side of the wood. The former were the re-formed chasseurs d'Afrique, which, themselves disordered by the charge as foragers on the battery of Captain von der Planitz, head to give way before the Prussian 13th Dragoons. Hostile *cuirassiers* were not present on this part of the battlefield. The *ulans* were probably deceived by the bright helmets with flowing plumes worn by the French dragoons, and it was perhaps the dragoons of De Clérembault's Division that they saw.
71. Bonie.

charge had been begun.[72] The enemy's horsemen pursued us at first, but, recalled by the trumpet, they reascended to the edge of the height; our men assembled and re-formed, covered on the left by the fire of the *chasseurs d'Afrique* and two companies of the 5th Battalion of Foot Chasseurs, which General Grenier had posted behind the trees along the road to Verdun[73] on the right by that of the horseless riders who had congregated on the edge of the wood, and by the 5th Battalion,[74] of the Foot Chasseurs who came from the Gréyère farmstead, and also by the fire of the 98th Regiment, posted in a wood between the road and the Gréyère farmstead; lastly, by the fire of the 12-pounders posted by General de Ladmirault to support the attack."

This description agrees on the whole with what the Prussian regiments engaged in this conflict state.

After a long and furious *mêlée*, which, according to some witnesses, lasted about half an hour, the enemy fled in disorder toward the wood, recalled, according to the French accounts, by the trumpet. The pursuing Prussian cavalry, itself in complete disorder, as any serious mounted conflict naturally entails for both sides, came under a cross-fire from the *chaussée* and from the wood. Major-General von Barby also had the recall sounded, and his regiments re-formed on the edge of the height southeast of Ville sur Yron.

Meanwhile General de Cléembault had brought up his division to the vicinity of the battlefield. He had not been informed of the advance of Generals Legrand and de France; it was only through the clouds of dust raised by the conflict that he became aware of the collision of the opposing masses of horse. He moved off at once to take part in the struggle. The *chasseur* regiments which formed his right wing, while in the act of descending into the ravine separating them from the field, were thrown in disorder and partially carried away by the hussars of De Montaigu's Brigade, which were hurrying to the rear in disorder.

The dragoon brigade of De Maubranches, the 4th regiment leading, alone succeeded in gaining the ground beyond. On the call of their colonel, "*À moi, dragons!*" the first squadron of the 4th Dragoons

---

72. North of the farmstead of Gréyère.

73. The *chaussée* from Jarny to Mars-la-Tour is probably the one meant.

74. Probably not more than four companies, two being posted on the road to Verdun.

threw itself on the last Prussian horsemen and cut them down.

The latter were probably such only as had been delayed near the wood of Gréyère by the exhaustion of their horses or other causes, for, although all the Prussian regiments report unanimously the appearance of fresh cavalry regiments of the enemy on the field just quitted, they state with equal unanimity that these regiments made no attempt to pursue, although the rallying and re-forming of the Prussians took quite a long time, as all the regiments had become completely intermixed. The 13th Dragoons, which were the first to be in line, and, having acted as the advance guard before the fight, now formed the rear guard and remained near Ville sur Yron until dark, state particularly in their report that the fresh cavalry regiments of the enemy forming in their front made no attempts whatever to molest them.

Shells[75] falling among the regiments before they were completely re-formed prompted Major-General von Barby to withdraw out of range and closer to Mars-la-Tour.

The general reports, as characteristic of the whole conflict:

"The charges were ridden by the regiments with great gallantry and determination, and it is to be regretted *that the horses no longer possessed the requisite strength to ride* the charges with greater vehemence. The efforts of the day in *riding to and fro on the battle-field in deep soil and hilly terrain*, and the fatigues of the preceding days, *coupled with bivouacs*, had considerably impaired the strength of the horses."

All the regiments of the 5th Cavalry Division had been in the saddle since daybreak. An approximate measurement of the distances traversed in marching hither and thither in the deep soil of the hilly battlefield gives about four German miles. The last charge from the halting-place of the regiments north of the *chaussée* to Verdun to the farmstead of La Grange amounted to 3,000 paces on the air-line.

Facta loquutur!

None of the officers, and, so far as can be ascertained from the official returns of the regiments, but twenty-eight men, remained as prisoners in the enemy's hands; the latter left in the hands of the Prussian horsemen: one brigade general (De Montaigu) seriously wounded, one colonel (Du Part, of the Guard dragoons), several captains and lieutenants, and a considerable number of men and horses. Unfortunately, the exact figures are nowhere stated.

---

75. Probably from the 12-pounders which General de Ladmirault had ordered in action near the farmstead of Gréyère to support the attack of his cavalry.

The losses of the regiments differed, and, on the whole? were not inconsiderable:

ORGANIZATIONS.	Dead.			Wounded.			Missing.			Total.		
	Officers.	Men.	Horses.	Officers.	Men.	Horses.	Officers.	Men.	Horses.	Officers.	Men.	Horses.
Brigade Staff..........	...	...	...	2	...	...	...	...	...	2	...	...
13th Dragoons.........	1	4	12	7	74	35	...	12	9	8	90	58
19th Dragoons.........	4	10	...	8	94	...	...	9	95	12	113	95
4th Cuirassiers(2 Sqs.)..	...	5	20	3	12	...	...	25	...	3	42	20
13th Ulans (3 Sqs.)	1	6	24	6	36	19	...	9	18	7	51	61
10th Hussars (3 Sqs.)...	1	2	10	3	25	13	...	4	15	4	31	38
16th Dragoons..........	1	1	8	1	11	12	...	1	22	2	13	42
2d Dragoons (G'd, 2 Sqs.)	2	5	37	2	85	45	...	13	...	4	103	82
Total............	10	33	111	32	337	124	...	*73	159	42	443	391

Of these 73 missing, 28 returned subsequently from captivity, as appears from official papers; the remaining 45 returned in part during the next few days; the remainder must be considered as killed.

There were killed:

Of the 13th Dragoons, First Lieutenant Rogalla von Bieberstein.

Of the 19th Dragoons, First Lieutenant Zedelius; the Second Lieutenants von Luck, Count von Lüttichau,, and von Unger.

Of the 13th Ulans, Colonel and Regimental Commander von Schack.

Of the 10th Hussars, Major von Hertell.

Of the 16th Dragoons, Second Lieutenant von Koblinski.

Of the 2nd Dragoons of the Guard, Colonel and Regimental Commander Count von Finkenstein and Captain von Hindenburg.

Thus 1 officer was killed to 3 men, while the organization provides 1 officer to 26 men.

At Mars-la-Tour the 16th Dragoons left the other regiments, with the exception of the 13th Dragoons, guarding the front dismounted, and went in quest of its infantry division (20th), taking with them at the same time the prisoners and delivering them at the headquarters of the 10th Corps.

On reaching Tronville, a general staff officer of the 3rd Corps asked the regiment to advance in the direction of Rézonville, in order to reap the fruits of the success gained there by the 3rd Corps.

With the 4th squadron in front as advance guard, the regiment trotted off in the direction indicated, but soon met the 9th Dragoons and several battalions and batteries, which delayed the advance. As no great success could be hoped for, since darkness intervened, the 4th squadron, under Captain von Kutzschenbach, was recalled and the regiment withdrawn to Tronville.

The squadron named had reached Rézonville, encountering there hostile infantry at the edge of the village and in the ditches by the roadside, from which it received a brisk fire. The squadron withdrew with a loss of 4 men wounded and 10 horses dead, and arrived at the regimental bivouac near Tronville at 9:30 p. m.[76]

As darkness settled down, Major-General von Barby ordered his other regiments also farther to the rear, and they went into bivouac: 4th Cuirassiers, 13th Ulans, 19th Dragoons, and 10th Hussars at Xonville; 13th Dragoons at Puxieux, as also the 5th squadron of the 2nd Dragoons of the Guard.

The detached squadrons of the 4th Cuirassiers and 13th Ulans rejoined their regiments here.

The latter (the 3rd squadron of the 13th Ulans, detached from Mars-la-Tour to the 19th Infantry Division) had assisted in rallying the dispersed men of the 38th (Von Wedell's) Infantry Brigade, and lost in doing so: dead, 2 men, 7 horses; wounded, 3 men; missing, 3 men; total, 8 men, 7 horses.

The 3rd squadron of the 2nd Dragoons of the Guard had been detailed as escort to General of Infantry von Voigts-Rhetz, and, when dismissed by him, it sought vainly for its brigade, and finally settled down at a dressing station south of Mars-la-Tour. The 4th squadron of the regiment succeeded in finding the 1st Dragoons of the Guard near Xonville, where the 2nd squadron also arrived later on.[77]

The remnants of the two regiments of the 12th Brigade, 7th Cuirassiers and 16th Ulans, had assembled southwest of Flavigny in the bottom extending toward the farmstead of Sauley. In the evening they went into bivouac south of Xonville.

During the events last described Major-General von Redern had maintained his position near Flavigny with the 11th and 17th Hussars, until the infantry combat in the Tronville copses became so brisk that it almost looked as though the battle, which opposite Rézonville had died down, was to recommence. The brigade therefore moved closer to Tronville, so as to be ready for any emergency. Here it met the 6th

---

76. This movement against Rézonville was therefore probably simultaneous with the advance of the 6th Cavalry Division against the same place.

77. The 5th squadron of the regiment had joined the 13th Dragoons near Puxieux.

Cavalry Division. After dark the commanding general of the 10th Army Corps permitted the brigade to go to the great road to water and feed the horses.

As the day declined, the battle gradually died out. Exhaustion descended on the blood-stained fields. Suddenly the battle recommenced. Brisk infantry fire resounded from the Prussian right, from the woods of St. Arnould and Des Ognons.

His Royal Highness Prince Frederick Charles, who had reached the battlefield after noon, deemed the moment opportune for bringing about a decision by a last general attack. The participation therein of the cavalry also seemed opportune now before darkness settled down. The 6th Cavalry Division, which had remained between Flavigny and Tronville, received orders:

> Grüter's Brigade to attack Rézonville in two lines in a fanshaped formation; Ranch's Brigade to accompany the right of the attack to be made along the *chaussée* by the 6th Infantry Division.

By this time the 14th Brigade had moved to the right and taken position in rear of the corps artillery of the 3rd Corps, because it looked as though the enemy were assembling large bodies of cavalry at Rézonville. In pursuance of the above order the brigade advanced north of, and following the direction of, the road Chambley—Rézonville against the enemy's position south of the village named.

The 3rd and 4th squadrons of the 3rd Ulans, in extended line of squadrons in platoon columns, were in first line. In second line, in similar formation and overlapping both flanks of the first line, were, on the right the 15th Ulans, on the left three squadrons of the 6th Cuirassiers; the brigade was accompanied on the right by the 12th Dragoons.

Increasing darkness made it impossible to see more than twenty paces ahead. A deserted hostile camp was traversed, where piles of firewood, cooking-pots, etc., obstructed the movement. Major-General von Grüter and Colonel Count von der Groeben rode forward to reconnoitre, as the enemy in front could be heard, but not seen. Colonel Count von der Groeben believed he recognized before him a formed mass of infantry and was just about to charge, when Major-General von Grüter returned. He had received fire from the right from what he believed to be hostile skirmish lines. He therefore gave orders to attack these skirmish lines, and not the closed bodies in front, in order not to come between two fires.

The squadrons wheeled by platoons to the right and trotted in this direction until they were believed to be opposite the hostile lines, when the platoons wheeled to the left, formed line and charged at a gallop, the first platoon of the 3rd squadron of the 3rd Ulans being pushed forward as a right offensive flank.

Protected by a bank of earth, the hostile infantry allowed the *ulans* to approach to within a few paces, when it opened a, most effective, rapid fire, which killed some forty horses at once. At the same time the squadrons received fire from their left from the closed infantry just mentioned, and had to retreat; when beyond range, they faced again toward the enemy (who, however, did not follow them), remained halted, and posted outposts.

The enemy went into bivouac to the west and north of Rézon-ville.

The other two regiments of the 14th Brigade, as well as the 12th Dragoons, came in no further contact with the enemy, but suffered some losses from the enemy's fire.

Major-General von Grüter was seriously wounded and obliged to hand the command over to Colonel Count von der Groeben, who put the brigade into bivouac, southwest of Flavigny at 1 a. m., August 17th, the third squadron of the 15th Ulans furnishing the outposts.

The 12th Dragoons had left the brigade at 10 p. m. and gone into bivouac along the *chaussée* Gorze—Chambley, not far from the former place.

The 15th Brigade, under command of Colonel von Schmidt, and three squadrons of the 9th Dragoons had left the position taken up southwest of Flavigny after the charge in the afternoon, and advanced to Tronville and northward of this village in support of the 19th In-fantry Division. Withdrawing toward evening in a south-easterly di-rection, the brigade was in a fold of the ground east of the height 288 near Tronville, when at 7 p. m. it received a request from Lieutenant-General von Buddenbrock to cover his batteries at Vionville. The lat-ter had expended almost all their ammunition and the general feared a cavalry charge, which seemed to be in preparation at Rézonville, and had also been noticed by the corps artillery farther south, on which account the 14th Brigade was requested at the same time to advance in support of the artillery.

Colonel von Schmidt at once advanced in the desired direction with the 3rd Hussars and 9th Dragoons, the 16th Hussars remaining in their previous position.

When the two regiments reached Vionville soon afterward, the hostile cavalry was just disappearing behind the heights of Rézonville and could no longer be reached.

On returning slowly to its former position, the brigade received the order mentioned to make an attack with the 6th Infantry Division, north of the *chaussée* Vionville Rézonville against the enemy's positions near the latter place.

The brigade was halted at once; the 16th Hussars were brought up and posted on the right, the 3rd Hussars on the left. The heads of the two regiments, in line of squadrons in platoon columns with deploying intervals, started abreast from the road Vionville Gorze, the 9th Dragoons following in second line in the same formation.

Leaving burning Flavigny on the right, the brigade trotted forward south of the Rézonville *chaussée* and toward the village of that name. According to directions from the brigade commander, the 3rd Hussars were to cross to the north side of the road first, followed by the two left squadrons of the 16th Hussars. About 300 paces to the north of the *chaussée* dense masses of infantry became visible; in the dark it could not be discerned whether they were hostile or Prussian infantry. They were firing briskly in all directions, and their bullets fell also among the brigade. Colonel von Schmidt rode forward in person to ascertain how matters stood, and met an adjutant, who informed him that these were battalions of the 6th Infantry Division and threatened by the enemy's cavalry.

Colonel von Schmidt now at once moved the entire brigade to the north side of the *chaussée*; it passed through the infantry, deployed, and rode at a gallop against one of those dark masses, which had to be presumed to be that hostile cavalry; this body avoided the charge by moving to the right, and immediately afterward a severe infantry fire was opened at close range. Both hussar regiments were in the midst of hostile infantry; they rode through several extensive skirmish lines, the enemy throwing himself on the ground and rising and firing into the hussars' rear as soon as they had passed. In rear of these skirmish lines stood closed bodies. They were partly pierced, partly dispersed by the hussars. The hostile infantry scattered, but maintained an uninterrupted, very brisk fire while running to the rear.

Here the horse of the standard-bearer, non-commissioned officer Grotte, received two bullets and fell; two of the enemy's infantry reached for the standard, but, knocking them down with the staff of the standard and pulling up his horse and spurring it to a last effort, the brave non-commissioned officer saved the insignia entrusted to him, representative of glorious traditions, the palladium of the old renowned regiment.

The right flank support of the enemy, which was on a small eminence and remained untouched, fired several volleys into the whirling mass, causing considerable loss, particularly to the 3rd Hussars. Colonel von Schmidt, assisted by Captain Krell, who commanded the left squadron, gathered some fifty hussars and with them rode against the support. But the bold attempt to disperse it failed. In the darkness the enemy's position could not be clearly recognized, and, moreover, there was no force to the blow. The horses were exhausted, *having been under the saddle since 2:30 a. m. and without water and food during the day,* and the men, no matter how willing they were, were no better off.

Further success could not be hoped for; the enemy was everywhere retreating; the rally was sounded, and, after re-forming as best they could in the darkness,, the regiments marched back at a walk.

As they passed through their infantry, the hussars gave vent to their elation in a loud hurrah.

According to the statements of some captured officers, it was the 93rd Regiment of the Line and the 12th Battalion of the Foot Chasseurs that the hussars had encountered; they also stated that, on seeing the advance of the Prussians, their own cavalry had withdrawn in rear of the infantry.

According to French reports, *zouaves* of the Guard also took part in this interlude of the battle.

The 93rd Regiment of the Line was part of Colin's (2nd) Brigade of La Font de Villiers' (3rd) Division of the 6th. Corps (Canrobert's); the 12th Battalion of Foot Chasseurs belonged to Pouget's (1st) Brigade of Bataille's (2nd) Division of the 2nd. Corps (Frossard's). During the conflicts of the day the left and right flanks respectively of the corps named had come in touch at the Rézonville—Vionville *chaussée,* and it is therefore very possible that in the evening troops of both were together at the same place. The French accounts do not contain the slightest reference to the attack contemplated by the French cavalry.

With reference to this last conflict of the day, Fay writes:

Marshal Bazaine had the *zouaves* posted across the Rézonville road; General Bourbaki led forward his men and repulsed a cavalry charge made by the regiments of the Duke of Mecklenburg's Division.

Bonie says:

A last charge terminated this long series of conflicts. Night had come, the Prussian army was withdrawing, when on the left of our lines we heard the gallop of horsemen who were approaching at full speed. A regiment of red hussars breaks through (*traverse*) our infantry, but, recovering from their surprise, the *zouaves* threw themselves into the ditches along the road, and by their fire dispersed these troops, which could barely be discerned and whose attack disappeared without definite object (*sans but defini*).

Colonel von Schmidt was wounded.

The 16th Hussars went into bivouac near Vionville, posted outposts, and sent forward numerous patrols, which found the enemy's position back as far as Gravelotte.

The 3rd Hussars bivouacked farther to the rear, near Gorze (, and at the same place the three squadrons of the 9th Dragoons also bivouacked. They had followed the charge of the two hussar regiments on the left rear; receiving fire in front from a closed body of the enemy and in left flank from another such body at a range of 80 yards, they withdrew some distance and fronted the enemy. The same difficulties rendered futile a renewed attempt to advance, as complete darkness rendered any survey of the hostile position impossible.

In these night attacks the two brigades had traversed, from the starting-point to the point of collision with the enemy, the 14th Brigade about 3,000, the 15th Brigade about 2,500 paces. The losses of both were considerable, particularly of the 3rd Hussars. Two officers, Captain von Grimm and Second Lieutenant von Klenke, were killed; three were wounded.

As the reports of the regiments do not exhibit separate lists of losses for this conflict, we must refer to the table of losses given below.

The 2nd Dragoons, which had been attached to the 6th Infantry Division, had had no opportunity to take part in any of the large cavalry charges; its actual employment, however, is not uninstructive as regards the use of divisional cavalry, and merits to find a place in the discussion of the employment of cavalry on this memorable day.

When the 6th Infantry Division marched off at 5 a. m., this regiment marched at the head. From Buxières large hostile camps became visible east of Vionville on both sides of the *chaussée*. The patrols thrown out reported that they had been received with brisk fire by the infantry encamped there. For the purpose of further reconnaissance, the 3rd squadron (Captain von Jagow) was dispatched toward Vionville, the 2nd (Captain von Cramm) toward Tronville. On reaching the *plateau*, the former received a brisk fire, retired into the wood of Gaumont, joined temporarily the 14th Cavalry Brigade, which advanced through that wood, and rejoined the regiment at 10 a. m.

The 2nd squadron advanced northward beyond Tronville, crossed the *chaussée* west of Vionville, and obtained a view of the enemy's position from the height on the north of this place. It appeared from this point as though part of the enemy was still in camp near Rézonville and as though strong columns were already in motion toward Vionville. This squadron also rejoined the regiment at 10 a. m.

During the further advance of the division the 1st squadron (Captain von Bothmer) was assigned to the advance guard, and there received orders to escort the artillery.

The 4th squadron (Captain von Kraatz-Koschlau) remained with the main body of the division. In the vicinity of Tronville it was joined by the 2nd and 3rd squadrons. These three squadrons received orders from Colonel von Voigt-Rhetz, chief of staff of the 3rd Corps, to protect the main body of the artillery; they consequently took up a position southwest of Vionville, to the right rear of the 6th Infantry Division and connected with the 5th Infantry Division. From this point the squadrons conformed in their movements forward to those of the batteries entrusted to their protection.

The 1st squadron made a short attack, passing between Vionville and the cemetery to support the hussar regiments of the 13th Brigade, returning from pursuit of the *cuirassiers* of the French Guard. They advanced into the enemy's infantry fire, but, finding no longer an opportunity to cut into the enemy, returned to the regiment.

Soon after 3 p. m., when the 20th and 21st Infantry Regiments were driven out of the Tronville copses on the north of the *chaussée* by the attack of Leboeuf's corps, the 2nd Dragoons were sent toward them in support. The latter crossed the great *chaussée* in front of the copses. The 1st squadron attempted to advance along the eastern edge of the copses to check the enemy's brisk pursuit, but the attempt failed through the too severe fire of the enemy's infantry, which, moreover, could not be reached in the dense undergrowth. The squadron withdrew slowly toward the regiment, which had remained halted on the *chaussée*.

Subsequently, when the 20th Infantry Division again advanced against the Tronville copses, the 4th squadron was detached to cover the horse batteries of the 10th Corps, which were in action near Tronville under Major von Koerber. The regiment took position in the bottom between Vionville and Tronville, was afterward brought up to the support of the corps artillery of the 10th Corps, and joined in the evening in the night attack of the 15th Cavalry Brigade, but, remaining south of the *chaussée*, it failed to become engaged. It finally went into bivouac southwest of Vionville.

COMPARISON OF STRENGTH AND LOSSES ON BOTH SIDES.

It is not uninteresting to briefly compare the bodies of cavalry present on the battlefield on both sides, their effectives and losses, which latter, unfortunately, can be accurately given only for the Prussians.

The calculation of effectives on the Prussian side is based on the average strength of 560 horses per regiment, as given in the return of the 11th of August.

With reference to the French regiments, as to whose strength and losses accurate details are lacking, it has been assumed that on the morning of August 16th the Guard and light regiments numbered 5 squadrons each and the heavy and line regiments 4 squadrons each, and that the squadrons numbered 100 horses.

There were present on the battlefield

　　　1. On the Prussian side:

3 *Cuirassier* regiments	1,680 horses.
3½ *Ulan* regiments	1,960 horses.
8 Dragoon regiments	4,480 horses.
4¾ Hussar regiments	2,660 horses.

Total, 19¼ regiments, with	10,780 horses.

　　　2. On the French side:

6 regiments of the Guard	3,000 horses.
2 *Cuirassier* regiments	800 horses.
10 Dragoon regiments	4,000 horses.
1 Lancer regiment	400 horses.
6 *Chasseur* regiments	3,000 horses.
2 1-5 Hussar regiments	1,100 horses.

Total, 27 1-5 regiments with	12,300 horses.

Of the French regiments the following were not engaged:

2 regiments of the Guard   1,000 horses.
3 Dragoon regiments   1,200 horses.
2-5 of one Chasseur regiment   200 horses.

_____

Total, 5 2-5 regiments, with   2,400 horses.

Leaving as actually engaged 21 4-5 regiments, with 9,900 horses.

If we deduct on the Prussian side those squadrons of the 17th Hussars and 9th and 12th Dragoons which did not take part in the cavalry combats proper—*viz.*, 3¾ squadrons, with 525 horses, there remain 18¾ regiments, with 10,255 horses.

There were thus employed on the Prussian side 355 horses more than on the French, although the latter had 1,520 horses more present, but did not employ them.

The Prussian losses were as follows:

ORGANIZATIONS.	Killed.			Wounded.			Missing.			Total.		
	Officers.	Men.	Horses.	Officers.	Men.	Horses.	Officers.	Men.	Horses.	Officers.	Men.	Horses.
Staff 11th Brigade	...	...	...	2	...	...	...	...	...	2	...	...
4th Cuirassiers	...	16	29	6	44	25	...	25	10	6	85	64
13th Ulans	1	6	24	6	36	19	...	9	18	7	51	61
19th Dragoons	4	10	...	8	94	...	...	9	95	12	113	95
7th Cuirassiers	1	43	33	6	72	25	...	83	203	7	198	261
16th Ulans	2	28	172	5	101	28	2	54	...	9	183	200
13th Dragoons	1	4	12	6	74	35	..	12	41	7	90	88
Staff 13th Brigade	...	...	...	1	...	...	...	...	...	1	...	...
10th Hussars	1	2	10	3	23	13	...	4	15	4	29	38
17th Hussars	...	8	74	2	68	...	...	14	...	2	90	74
11th Hussars	...	1	..	...	19	...	...	2	30	...	22	30
Staff 14th Brigade	...	...	.	1	...	...	..	...	...	1	...	...
6th Cuirassiers	...	...	4	1	6	5	...	...	...	1	6	9
3d Ulans	...	7	24	1	16	20	...	2	33	1	25	77
15th Ulans	...	6	18	3	24	12	..	2	4	3	32	34
Staff 15th Brigade	...	...	1	1	...	...	...	...	...	1	...	1
3d Hussars	2	28	145	6	80	34	...	50	32	8	158	211
16th Hussars	1	5	11	2	27	61	...	...	...	3	32	72
1st Guard Dragoons	5	43	204	6	78	42	...	5	...	11	126	246
2d Guard Dragoons	2	7	107	5	112	45	...	13	...	7	132	152
2d Dragoons	...	2	16	1	11	10	..	...	...	1	13	26
9th Dragoons	...	...	6	...	9	6	...	1	2	...	10	14
12th Dragoons	...	...	28	...	13	4	..	...	...	...	13	32
16th Dragoons	1	1	18	1	15	12	...	1	22	2	17	52
Total	21	217	936	73	922	398	2	286	505	96	1425	183 7

One officer was killed to every 10 men; in the grand total 1 officer was lost to every 15 men.

Of the field strength, there was lost every seventh man and sixth horse. The total strength of the Prussian forces engaged on the 16th of August amounted to 67,000 men, of which 10,780 horses formed about the sixth part. The cavalry, therefore, bore its full share of the losses of the day. These losses amounted altogether to 640 officers and 15,170 men; of the cavalry, 96 officers and 1,425 men.

In the total losses, therefore, there was 1 cavalry officer to every 6 officers lost, and 1 horseman to every 10 men lost.

These are proportions which will probably not often be repeated in the annals of war, and which furnish positive proof that the cavalry is entitled to claim a full share of the successful result of the day.

www.ingramcontent.com/pod-product-compliance
Lightning Source LLC
Chambersburg PA
CBHW021108090426
42738CB00006B/559